John William Griffith

An Elementary Textbook of the Microscope

John William Griffith

An Elementary Textbook of the Microscope

ISBN/EAN: 9783744689519

Printed in Europe, USA, Canada, Australia, Japan

Cover: Foto ©Andreas Hilbeck / pixelio.de

More available books at **www.hansebooks.com**

AN

ELEMENTARY TEXT-BOOK

OF

THE MICROSCOPE;

INCLUDING A DESCRIPTION OF THE METHODS OF
PREPARING AND MOUNTING OBJECTS, ETC.

BY

J. W. GRIFFITH, M.D., F.L.S., ETC.,

MEMBER OF THE ROYAL COLLEGE OF PHYSICIANS; CONJOINT AUTHOR OF
THE MICROGRAPHIC DICTIONARY, ETC.

WITH TWELVE COLOURED PLATES,
CONTAINING 451 FIGURES.

LONDON:
JOHN VAN VOORST, PATERNOSTER ROW.
MDCCCLXIV.

PREFACE.

THE object of this little work is to furnish an elementary course of instruction in the use of the Microscope, and on its application to the examination of the structure of plants and animals. Assuming that the reader has had no previous acquaintance with the Microscope, or with the study of natural history, I have attempted to render the descriptions of the objects as simple as possible. At the same time, the technical terms have been added and explained, in order gradually to render them familiar to the reader, and thus facilitate the future study of larger and more detailed works. The objects figured and described comprise the principal structures and more minute forms of both the vegetable and the animal kingdom, those having been selected which are common and readily procurable.

A chapter has been given upon the optical prin-

ciples on which the action of the instrument depends
(which will assist the reader to understand the opera-
tion of its constituent parts), including a sketch of
the subject of polarized light. The order in which
the subjects are treated is scientific, and particular
directions have been given for the examination of
the objects.

The small size of the work has necessitated the
exclusion of figurative descriptions, so that it is
adapted rather for a worker than a reader; at the same
time, the matter forms a course, and must be taken
as a whole for the proper comprehension of the subjects. The technical terms used are referred to in
the Index, so as to furnish to some extent a glossary
of terms; and their derivation is given, to facilitate
their recollection. The figures, with very few exceptions, are drawn from nature, and are coloured that
the objects may be more easily recognized. The
magnifying powers under which they have been drawn
are denoted by a small number placed beneath each
figure: and the particular attention of the reader is
requested to this point; otherwise the whole subject
will be utterly confused; so much does the appearance
of objects vary under different powers.

Directions are given for preparing and mounting

objects, implying that the reader will collect specimens for himself, which is to be strongly recommended as the best method of acquiring a practical and useful acquaintance with the objects. These will serve to furnish permanent landmarks in the great ocean of structural forms, will probably recall in after-years pleasant recollections of early excursions in search of the beauties of nature, and, surely, deepen the conviction of the existence of their All-wise Creator.

J. W. G.

CONTENTS.

PLATE I. [FRONTISPIECE.]

VEGETABLE TISSUES, &C.

Fig.
1. Leaf of Geranium : cells, chlorophyll, and intercellular passages.
2. Cells of Apple.
3. Starch-granules : *a*, of Wheat; *b*, of Arrowroot; *c*, of Potato; *d*, of Oat; *e*, of Lentil; *f*, of Rice.
4. Cells of Potato, containing Starch.
5. Garden Rhubarb-stalk : *a*, raphides; *b*, reticulated duct; *c*, spiral vessel; *d*, woody fibre; *e*, annular vessel.
6. Wood-cells from stem of Chrysanthemum.
7. Deal, transverse section : *a*, glandular tissue; *b*, woody fibre.
8. Deal, longitudinal (radial) section of glandular tissue.
9. Deal, longitudinal section of woody fibre.
10. Deal, tangential section.
11. Holly, wood of : *a*, porous cells; *b, d, e*, wood-cells; *c*, dotted ducts.
12. Hairs, vegetable : *a, b*, of Groundsel; *c*, of London Pride; *d, e*, of Geranium; *f*, of Chrysanthemum.
13. Epidermis of Geranium-leaf.
14. Style of Crocus, with pollen-granule and -tube.
15. Pollen-grain of Crocus, with pollen-tube.
16. Pollen of Primrose.
17. Pollen of Sunflower.
18. Pollen of *Convolvulus major*.
19. Caraway-seed.
20. Needle-point.
21. Sting of Nettle.
22. Hair of Spiderwort.
23. Hair of Spiderwort, single cell.

Fig.
24. Epidermis of Geranium-petal.
25. Petal of Chickweed.
26. Sepal of Chickweed.
27. Seed of Poppy.
28. Epidermis of *Deutzia*.
29. Seed of Mignonette.
30. Pollen of Chickweed, dry.
31. Pollen of Chickweed, in water.
32. Flower of Chickweed.
33. Epidermis of petal of Chickweed.
34. Hairs of calyx of Chickweed.
35. Hairs of seed of *Collomia*.
36. Stem of Dicotyledon, section of.
37. Stem of Monocotyledon, section of.
38. Seed of Shepherd's Purse, transverse section.
39. Stamen of Chickweed.
40. Stigma of Chickweed.
41. Ovary of Chickweed.
42. Leaf of Chickweed.
43. Seed of Wallflower, section of.
44. Seed of Wallflower, radicle and cotyledons.
45. Embryo-sac of Chickweed.
46. Embryo-sac of Chickweed.
47. Embryo-sac of Chickweed.
48. Wheat, cotyledon and leaves of, section.
49. Mustard-seed, cotyledons and radicle.
50. Mustard-seed, transverse section.
51. Chickweed, seed of.
52. Seed of *Eccremocarpus scaber*.
53. Grain of Wheat : *a*, cotyledon; *b*, embryo; *c*, radicle; *d*, albumen.
54. Ovule of Wallflower.
55. Cotyledons of Chickweed.
56. Plum-stone, section of.

A

TEXT-BOOK

OF

THE MICROSCOPE.

CHAPTER I.

THE MICROSCOPE.

THE microscope (from μικρὸς, little, and σκοπέω, to
see), so called because it enables us to see objects
which are too small to be seen with the naked eye,
consists of several parts, each of which has its special
use. As the proper management of these is of great
importance in the successful application of the instrument to minute investigations, we shall com-
mence with the consideration of their names and
uses, including those of the more important pieces of
accessory apparatus.

Microscope.—The foot of the microscope is that
part which supports the instrument upon the table;
it is connected above with the stand, of which it is
often considered a part. The stand sometimes consists of a single rod or pillar; but in the best microscopes it is composed of two upright plates, between
which, at the upper part, the rest of the microscope
swings stiffly upon an axle. Arising from this axle,
indirectly through the medium of parts which require
no special mention, is an arm, to which the body is

fixed. The body is moveable up and down by one or two large milled heads, connected with a grooved rod or pinion, which works in the teeth of a rack fixed to the back of the body, or of the arm which supports the body. The large milled heads form the " coarse movement," as it is called.

On the top of the arm, or on the front and lower part of the body of the microscope, is placed the " fine movement," consisting of a small milled head, with a fine screw, for moving the body through very small distances.

Next is the " stage," or flat plate, upon which the objects to be viewed are placed. This is often so arranged that, by turning two milled heads, the object can be moved backwards and forwards, or from side to side; it is then a " moveable stage."

The eye-piece slides into the upper end of the body; and the object-glass screws into its lower end.

Beneath the stage is the mirror, which reflects the light through the object, the object-glass, and eye-piece to the eye.

Object-glasses.—The object-glasses are the most valuable parts of the instrument. There are generally three or more of them; and, by means of an " adapter," any object-glass can be made to fit any microscope. Great care is required in their use, especially to avoid scratching the lower surface of the glass, which is sometimes accidentally done by pressing the surface against any hard body, or allowing such a body to fall upon it. When not in use, the object-glasses should either be put away in the brass boxes or covered with a small bell-glass, to prevent their receiving any injury.

The object-glasses possess various magnifying powers, according to the distance at which they require to be placed from the object for distinct vision: this is not, however, absolutely correct, yet may serve as a general expression. Thus we have a

1-inch, ½-inch, ¼-inch object-glass, &c. The object-glasses, for brevity, are often called powers.

As a beginner may at first have some difficulty in distinguishing a high from a low power, it may be remarked that the size of the lower glass is larger the lower the power: but, in the case of the better object-glasses, the focal distance is engraved on the box in which the object-glass is packed when put away.

As the coarse movement raises or depresses the body and object-glass through comparatively large distances, it must be used only with the lower object-glasses, *i. e.* those of low or little magnifying power, as the 2-inch, 1-inch, or ½-inch, or to bring the object-glass near the focal distance with the higher powers; whereas the fine movement serves to adjust the higher powers, as the ¼-inch, &c.

If the object-glasses should become soiled on the lower face, this should be wiped very gently with an old silk handkerchief or piece of very soft wash-leather, previously shaken to displace dust. The same method will answer to cleanse the upper surface of the eye-piece.

Great care must be taken that a slide which has been warmed in any experiment be not placed near the object-glass until quite cold.

Mirror.—The mirror has sometimes one silvered face only, at others two—one flat, the other concave. The flat surface is used to reflect the light upon the object when the light is too great with the concave surface.

Beneath the stage, in most microscopes, is a circular moveable "diaphragm," perforated with holes of various sizes, to allow more or less of the light reflected by the mirror to pass through, as may be required.

When opake objects are viewed, the mirror should

be turned aside, so as not to reflect any light through the stage.

Eye-pieces.—With all microscopes, two or more eye-pieces are supplied. These possess different magnifying powers, and are lettered or numbered accordingly; the lowest power with the earliest letters of the alphabet, or with the smallest numbers, thus: A, B, C; or 1, 2, 3, &c.

Forceps.—These are fine pincers, for holding minute bodies to be viewed as opake objects. In use, they are inserted by a stem connected with a joint, in an aperture, generally in the stage; and are moveable in all directions.

Live-box.—This is a brass slide, perforated in the middle, to the aperture in which is soldered a short piece of brass tube, closed at the top with a circular plate of thin glass. A rather wider and longer piece of brass tube slides over the former; this is also closed at the top by a thin glass plate, so as to allow of an object being confined or compressed between the two glass plates. It is used for examining living objects in water.

Knife, &c.—For cutting slices or sections of objects, a very sharp knife with a thin back will be found useful; or a razor may be used for the same purpose. And for picking minute objects to pieces, or dissection, fine needles, cut off short with pliers, the blunt ends being thrust into hair-pencil sticks, will be requisite.

A pair of fine surgical forceps will also be required, for taking up minute objects. These should be without teeth, and the spring-action so weak that the points can be very easily approximated.

Dipping-tubes.—For removing minute objects from water, two or three narrow glass tubes, of different lengths, are very useful. These are called "dipping tubes," and are used thus:—the tube being held upright between the second finger and the thumb, the fore finger is placed at the top of the tube to close it; the tube is then put into the water until the lower end is close to the object, when, on suddenly removing the fore finger, the water will rise in the tube, carrying the object with it. The fore finger is then again applied to the tube, and, as thus held, the water will not run out. The tube is then held over a watch-glass, or a slide, upon which the water and object will fall on removing the fore finger.

A small glass spirit-lamp will be found very useful. The spirit for burning should be methylated alcohol, or wood-naphtha. As these spirits are inflammable, great care should be taken to keep the stock-bottle away from a candle or other flame, when filling the lamp.

Achromatic condenser.—A very important piece of apparatus, when high powers are used, is the achromatic condenser; it is not, however, usually supplied with the cheaper microscopes. It consists of a brass fitting, placed beneath the stage, into which an object-glass is screwed, in an inverted position, *i. e.* the small end of the object-glass being placed uppermost. It serves to condense the light to a focus upon the object, so as to illuminate it more brightly; and as it can be elevated or depressed by a milled head and rack-work, the object can be viewed by either converging or diverging rays.

Simple microscope. — For examining the larger kinds of objects, and for dissection, a simple microscope is very useful. This consists of a stand, a stage, and an arm supporting a simple lens or combination of lenses, but without the body of the compound microscope (as the ordinary microscope is distinctively called). For most purposes, common plano-convex or doubly convex lenses are sufficient to form the object-glasses of a simple microscope. With the best microscopes, an "erector," or tube containing a pair of lenses, fitted within the body, renders the compound microscope capable of answering most of the purposes of a simple microscope.

Polariscope.—An expensive but interesting and useful addition to a microscope is a polarizing apparatus, or polariscope. This consists of a Nicol's prism, or a plate of tourmaline, placed beneath the stage, and another in the body of the microscope or above the eye-piece; both in brass fittings. The former is called the polarizer, and the latter the analyzer.

Rotating disk.—Another most useful piece of apparatus, for moving opake objects whilst under the microscope, in all directions, is Smith and Beck's "rotating disk."

Slides.—The slides upon which objects, especially those to be viewed as transparent objects, are to be placed, should be made of crown or plate glass. They are usually 3 inches long, and 1 inch wide; but I prefer them $2\frac{1}{2}$ inches long, and 1 inch wide, simply because they take up less room in a cabinet, and because they do not project beyond the stage on either side. They should not be more than $\frac{1}{20}$th of an inch thick, and as colourless and clear as possible. The edges should be ground or filed, to prevent their scratching the stage.

Covers.—The covers are square pieces of very thin glass, less in breadth than the slides, so as not to reach their margins; and of various thicknesses, the thicker and stronger being used to cover large objects for examination under the lower powers, and the thinner serving to cover very delicate objects requiring the higher powers.

Side condenser.—For illuminating opake objects, a large plano-convex or doubly convex "bull's-eye" lens, or side condenser, is used; this is fixed to an arm, which slides on a stand, so as to be capable of being raised or lowered to a suitable height. This is placed between the source of light and the stage, and at such a distance from the latter that the light may be brought to a focus upon the object. Sometimes a " Lieberkuhn " or concave silver reflector is used for this purpose.

These are the most important pieces of apparatus required in examining microscopic bodies. But the beginner will do well, if he have the achromatic condenser and the polarizing apparatus, to lay these aside until he has had considerable practice in examining objects simply with the mirror and the lower powers.

General method of observation.—In the ordinary use of the microscope, the object to be examined is laid upon the middle of a slide, which is placed upon the stage. The object is then brought under the centre of the object-glass, the mirror inclined half towards the light and half towards the object, until the object is seen to be illuminated, when, upon looking through the eye-piece and adjusting the coarse and fine movements, the object as it comes into focus will be seen, as it were, drawn upon a white disk, which is called the " field."

When the object is wet, it cannot be viewed without the application of a cover, because the water evaporates and condenses upon the under surface of the object-glass.

To avoid the danger of injuring the object-glass, or crushing the object by lowering the body and object-glass too much in adjustment to focus, the best plan is to lower the body by means of the coarse movement until the object-glass appears near the object to the eye placed on one side of the stage, and then to apply the eye to the eye-piece, and turn the milled head so as to raise the body and object-glass until the object is brought into focus.

In the examination of an object, it is best to begin with a low power, so as to obtain a view of the general arrangement of its parts, and then to apply the higher eye-pieces and powers, so that the more minute structural details may be observed.

Illumination.—The illumination or proper management of the light in using the microscope is of very great importance. The best light, especially with the low powers, is daylight, particularly that reflected from white clouds; this is least injurious to the eyes. But as daylight cannot always be used for microscopic investigations, and as cloud-light is insufficient with the higher powers, some kind of artificial light must be supplied. That mostly used is the light of a reading oil lamp or of a gas-burner, a candle being quite useless, on account of the flickering of the flame with the slightest draught. A moderator lamp has the defect of too great height; otherwise this would be better than any other oil lamp. A powerful and excellent light for the highest powers is afforded by a short paraffine-oil lamp.

As intently looking at strongly illuminated objects is injurious to the sight, the amount of light allowed to pass the diaphragm should be no more than is agreeable, and sufficient to show the object distinctly.

In using the higher powers, the field is much less bright with the use of the same light than in the case of the lower powers; and difficulty is often found in obtaining sufficient light for the distinct vision of the object. The achromatic condenser is of most important service here; but it is sometimes requisite, even when this is used, to condense the light upon the mirror by a shallow bull's-eye; or a large common metallic reflector may be used for the same purpose.

The most convenient manner of proceeding in regard to the use of the individual eyes is to apply the left eye to the eye-piece, so that the right eye may be used in finding the stage-movements, or in moving the slide, without removing the eye from the eye-piece. If this arrangement be adopted, the light should be placed towards the left-hand side of the microscope. But the best way to avoid injuring the sight would be to use both eyes for viewing the objects in turn, although most microscopic observers make use of one eye only for this purpose.

The structure of many transparent objects can be best seen when the mirror is turned more or less obliquely to one side, so as to view them by oblique light, as it is called : we shall refer to this point hereafter.

As a rule, objects are best seen by transmitted light, or as transparent objects, although it is well to examine objects under both kinds of illumination, *i. e.* by transmitted and reflected light.

If during the use of the microscope, after removing the eye from the instrument, the impression of the light remains perceptible to the sight, the light used has been too strong, or its action too long continued; and the instrument should be at once laid aside for a time.

CHAPTER II.

THE MOUNTING OF OBJECTS.

THE mounting or "putting up" of microscopic objects signifies their preparation in such way that they may be preserved for future reference and observation.

As a general rule, objects should be mounted in that manner by which their structure is best and most clearly shown; but in certain instances the objects are mounted so as to make their structure difficult of detection, that they may form test-objects of the power and quality of the microscope.

Some objects require to be mounted in the dry state, while others are best mounted in liquid; some again as opake, others as transparent objects: these must be considered separately.

Dry opake objects were formerly mounted by gumming them upon small coin-shaped pieces or disks of cork, blackened upon the surface with a mixture of fine lamp-black and thin warm size, laid on with a hair-pencil. They were kept in a drawer, to the bottom of which a sheet of cork was glued, the disk being transfixed by the pin, so that the free or projecting pointed end of the pin could be thrust into the sheet-cork. This plan may still be adopted in the case of common objects, as seeds, &c.; but it is objectionable, on account of the facility with which the bare objects are knocked off or injured by dust.

Hence dry opake objects are usually mounted in such manner as to be enclosed in a cell, the sides being formed by a ring of glass-tube or cork, or a square piece of leather, cardboard, or paper, with a hole cut or punched out of the middle. The glass rings are best; but as they are expensive, some of the other substances are generally used. The size and thickness of the material from which the rings are made must obviously vary according to the size and depth of the object. The rings are cemented to the middle of ordinary slides; and it is best to keep a number of them ready prepared. The cementing material must vary according to the nature of the ring used. If this consists of glass, Canada-balsam or marine glue is best. In using the former, the ring is gently heated over the flame of the spirit-lamp, and a thin layer of the balsam applied to its upper or under surface, by means of an iron wire with a little balsam on its end; it is next warmed over the spirit-lamp, so that the surface is entirely and evenly coated. A clean slide is then slightly heated, the ring laid upon it, and gentle pressure is used to squeeze out the excess of balsam; and the slide is kept at a gentle heat, until on cooling the balsam becomes so hard as not to be indented with the finger-nail. Marine glue is applied in the same way as the balsam, except that prolonged heat is not required to harden it, for it becomes hard on cooling. The balsam may also be replaced by black japan or asphalte.

The pieces of cork, leather, or paper are best fastened to the slides with solution of shellac or sealing-wax in methylated alcohol, or with white hard varnish.

When the ring or piece has been firmly fixed to the slide by either of the above cementing materials, so as to form the sides of the cell, the bottom is to be covered with a piece of black paper, cut to fit it exactly, and fastened to the surface of the slide with a little gum, or of either of the above varnishes. As soon as this is thoroughly dry, the upper surface of the cell-wall, whether of glass or cork, &c., is thinly covered with varnish, and a clean thin-glass cover laid upon it, and very lightly pressed; the object is then permanently preserved.

The main points to be observed are, that the object and varnish are completely dry, and that the cell is thoroughly closed. If the latter be not the case, more varnish must be applied to any little openings which may have been left; and it is better to apply the varnish in very small quantities at a time, the application being renewed as soon as the previous layer is quite dry.

Dry transparent objects are usually small and delicate; for, unless they are so, their structure cannot be well seen. In mounting these, a square piece of note-paper or tracing-paper, with the centre cut out, may be fastened to a clean slide with a little paste, gum, or shellac varnish. When this is thoroughly dry, the object is placed in the vacant space, a clean dry cover laid on, and the varnish applied by means of a hair-pencil to the edges in very small quantities. This will run in between the under surface of the edges of the cover and the upper surface of the paper, and when dry will cement the two together.

Supposing that the object is so delicate that it cannot be removed from the surface of a slide, if it will not be injured by heat, a good plan is to draw a square or circle around the object with a little black japan, then to heat the slide gradually until the japan is not indented with the finger-nail when cold. A clean slide is then laid upon the ring of japan, the whole again gently warmed, until the varnish is softened, and the cover lightly pressed so as to be in contact all round with the varnish. The slide must then be rapidly cooled, by being laid upon a piece of metal, which prevents the varnish from running in so as to spoil the object.

Many dry transparent objects can be preserved by mounting in Canada balsam. This is the best process for mounting objects in general; but only those can be so preserved which are not injured by drying, and which are not rendered too transparent by the balsam. If the object to be mounted in balsam be small, it is thoroughly dried, and then a drop of oil of turpentine added to it upon a slide; the slide is then gently warmed, which causes the turpentine to evaporate. When this has nearly all evaporated, a drop of balsam is allowed to fall upon the object from the end of a wire held at a distance above the flame of a spirit-lamp. A warmed cover is next laid upon the balsam, and gentle pressure applied until the cover is sufficiently depressed. The slide is then kept at a gentle heat until the balsam is quite hard when cold. The superfluous portions may be removed with the point of a knife, and any residues cleaned off with turpentine or a little benzole on a cloth.

Another way consists in laying a cover upon the dry object on a slide, adding a drop of turpentine, and warming the whole over a spirit-lamp until all air-bubbles are displaced, then continuing the application of the heat until most of the turpentine has evaporated. A drop or more of the balsam may next be applied to the edge of the cover, when it will run in and mix with the turpentine. The whole is then gently heated until the balsam is hard when cold, more balsam being added if necessary, to replace the turpentine which has evaporated.

When the objects are large, they should be pressed as flat as possible without injury between two slides, being retained until dry by enclosure between the prongs of an American clothes-peg; or the slides may be fastened at the ends by sealing-wax. When perfectly dry, the object should be immersed in turpentine, kept in a common gallipot, until all the air-bubbles have been entirely displaced, and the object appears very transparent. It is then removed from the turpentine with forceps, drained, laid upon a slide, and melted balsam dropped upon it until it is quite covered. A clean dry slide is then laid upon

c

its surface, and the two slides gently pressed together, the two slides fixed at the ends by sealing-wax, and the whole allowed to cool and dry. If requisite, more balsam is added to fill up any vacuities. When the balsam has become hard, the excess is cleaned away with a knife and turpentine, and the object is permanently mounted.

If the object should be spoiled by the presence of air-bubbles, the slides and object should be immersed in turpentine or methylated alcohol, until the whole of the balsam is dissolved; the remounting may then be proceeded with as at first. If the slides have been immersed in the alcohol (which is the quickest method), the object must be soaked in turpentine before the balsam is reapplied.

If, after an object has been mounted in balsam, on applying heat, bubbles resembling air-bubbles should be formed, the object must not be considered as spoiled; for these are merely bubbles of the vapour of turpentine, and will disappear spontaneously after a little time.

A quick way of mounting in balsam is to drop the melted balsam at once upon the dried object; but as air-bubbles are very apt to be produced in this way, the beginner had better previously apply the turpentine.

As balsam is very viscid, and adheres firmly to everything with which it comes in contact, some care is required in its use. Young microscopists very generally manage to soil the microscope, tables, chairs, papers, books, and even their clothes with it. It may be easily cleaned off, however, with turpentine or benzole.

Moist objects are best preserved, whenever practicable, in glycerine. There are, however, two important objections to its use: one is, that it makes objects very transparent; the other is, that it often wrinkles and distorts them, by withdrawing their watery contents. Hence only those objects can be preserved in glycerine, which are not too transparent, and which are sufficiently firm to resist the tendency to collapse.

When the objects are tolerably flat, and sufficiently firm to bear the pressure of the cover, they may be mounted by adding a small quantity of glycerine to them lying on a slide; the cover is then applied, and a little of the cement mentioned below applied warm with a hair-pencil around the edges of the cover to fasten it to the slide. Care is required that the glycerine applied be no more than sufficient; for wherever it has touched the cover or the slide, the cement will not adhere. Superfluous portions may be sucked up with a piece of clean moist sponge or a corner of blotting-paper.

When it is required to mount a large number of objects in a short time, the cement need only be applied to two opposite sides of the cover, leaving the other two sides open.

When the objects require to be protected from the pressure of the cover, the sides of a cell must be made with the cement or black japan upon the slide before the cover is applied, a further quantity being used to close the cell as usual.

A very strong solution of chloride of calcium may be used for the same purposes and in the same way as the glycerine. It has the advantage of not making the object so transparent; but it has the disadvantage of crystallizing slightly in a dry atmosphere. In most cases, I prefer it to glycerine.

A large number of interesting objects cannot, however, be preserved in either glycerine or chloride of calcium, without their value being impaired by the cause mentioned above. Many kinds of liquid have been recommended for preserving these, all agreeing mainly in being inefficient. The objection to them is, that they are evaporable; and after the object has been mounted for some time, the liquid creeps between the cement and the slide or cover, at some spot, and evaporates; and if the cement be not quite hard, the inner and more liquid portion of it runs into the cell, and spoils the object. A solution, containing a grain of salt and a grain of alum to the ounce of distilled water, is as good as any other; or simply distilled water in which a piece of camphor has been kept. In use, the cell is first formed by making a circle or outline square on the slide with black japan, and heating this carefully until it becomes solid when cold. The object is then laid in the cell, the liquid added, and the cover applied, any excess being removed with blotting-paper. The cell is to be closed with old black japan or gold-size, applied round the margins of the cover with a hair pencil. A second and a third layer of the varnish may be applied upon the first, when it has become hard outside. Although black japan and gold-size are generally used for the cement, I prefer that mentioned below.

When large preparations are mounted in liquid, the cell-walls are either formed of glass rings, or they are built up with four oblong pieces of glass, cemented to the slide and to each other with marine glue. A very good preservative liquid for large specimens is a solution of chloride of zinc, in the proportion of 20 grains to the ounce of distilled water. A mixture of spirit of wine and water, in the proportion of 1 part to 2, or 1 to 4, is often used for the same purpose.

When preparations are mounted, the cement and the adjacent parts of the slide and cover should be coated with a solution of sealing-wax in spirit, which hardens the exterior of the cement.

The cement above alluded to is made by melting together 5 parts of rosin, 2 parts of balsam, 1 part of bees'-wax, and 1 of red ochre. The cement is best kept in a little metallic cup, and melted over a spirit-lamp when used. It should be applied while hot, with a hair pencil; and cools very quickly.

The preservative liquids should be kept in corked bottles, a hair pencil being fixed into the under part of the cork; or, what is better, in stoppered bottles, the stopper being prolonged to a point nearly reaching the bottom of the bottle.

As soon as the preparations are mounted, they should be labelled, the labels being kept ready gummed. The balsam should be kept in a capped bottle, such as is used for holding solutions of gum, with an iron wire for removing portions as required. By keeping, the balsam becomes thicker; it may be thinned by the addition of oil of turpentine, and the application of a gentle heat.

The black japan, &c., may be procured at any oilshop; the glass rings, cell-sides, covers, &c., from Mr. Norman, 178 City Road, or of the microscopemakers.

Mounted objects should be kept in shallow drawers, and be laid flat—not standing on edge.

Magnifying power.—Before entering upon the consideration of the objects themselves, a word or two must be said upon the magnifying powers. In the plates of this work, the serial number of each figure is expressed by large numerals placed above the objects, while the number of times the object is magnified is indicated by small numerals placed beneath. The latter must be understood to express the number of times the drawing is larger than the object in one dimension. Thus, considering fig. 13, Plate I. to be an inch in width (for it is really somewhat less), being magnified 150 times in the direction of the width, the object itself is about $\frac{1}{150}$th of an inch in size; and it is represented magnified 150 times linear, or 150 diameters, as it is called.

A knowledge of the number of times the object is magnified is of the greatest importance in making use of the drawings; for, without it, the observer will be unable to apply such a magnifying power of the microscope as will enable him to see the structural appearances figured in the drawings.

The observer must also be acquainted with the magnifying powers of his microscope with the various object-glasses and eye-pieces. These are usually given when the instrument is purchased. Or they may be determined approximatively thus :—An ivory scale, with $\frac{1}{100}$th of an inch engraved upon it, is placed on the stage, and viewed as an opake object, both eyes being kept open; and the size of the image of one of the gradations is measured with compasses, upon the stage as seen with that eye which is not applied to the eye-piece. The number of $\frac{1}{100}$ths of an inch contained in the measure obtained with the compasses represents the magnifying power. Thus, supposing the image of the $\frac{1}{100}$th of an inch on the scale appears magnified to the length of 1 inch on the stage; the magnifying power is 100 diameters, or 100 times linear. This proceeding is difficult to any one unaccustomed to the use of the microscope, yet by practice it becomes very easy. Other methods, which require the use of the camera lucida, are given in the Micrographic Dictionary.

CHAPTER III.

VEGETABLE ELEMENTS AND TISSUES.

WE may now enter upon the consideration of the microscopic structure of objects, beginning with those which are derived from the vegetable kingdom, as they are more easily procured and prepared for examination than those belonging to the animal kingdom; moreover they are not so transparent, and hence are more readily distinguished under the microscope, which is of importance in the case of an unpractised observer.

Cells.—The elements of which all plants consist are cells. Cells, in their simplest condition, are microscopic, rounded, colourless, closed sacs or vesicles, resembling small bladders (Plate I. fig. 2), and consist of a thin, transparent, colourless, vegetable skin or membrane (*a*) called the cell-wall. The cells are well seen in a little of the pulp of an apple (fig.2), or in a section of almost any soft part of a plant. A high power is usually required to show them distinctly, on account of their minute size. The outline of the cells is seen to be double, one line indicating the inner, the other the outer, surface of the cell-wall, the space between the two lines corresponding to the thickness of the cell-wall.

In the pulp of the apple, the cells are loosely connected, and so retain their rounded form; but in most parts of plants, the cells become crowded and squeezed together, from their ordinary or normal expansion being limited in certain directions, so as mutually to alter each other's shapes. The sides then lose their originally rounded form and outline, becoming more or less straight (Pl. I. figs. 1 & 4),—

the cells at the same time mostly adhering to each other, so as to be separated with difficulty.

The forms thus produced are various and interesting, and have all received names by which they are distinguished. They are described in works on botany in two ways—according to the outline (which is the most common, as this expresses the appearance usually presented in sections and on the surfaces of vegetable structures), or according to the entire or solid form, which it is often a difficult matter to determine.

Cellular tissue.—Cells aggregated thus form a tissue, which is called cellular tissue or *paren'chyma* (παρὰ, among, and ἔγχυμα, poured substance), because it fills up the interstices of the other tissues of plants.

In technical descriptions, the cell-structure is often left out of consideration; and bodies composed of parenchymatous tissue are described as being reticulated or netted, because the united sides of the cell-walls appear as a network covering the surface.

It must be understood that parenchymatous cells are such only as have the three dimensions of solidity (viz. the length, breadth, and depth) nearly equal.

Intercellular passages.—The observer will not have examined many sections of cellular tissue, without noticing certain irregular black lines running between the cells, as in a piece of a Geranium- (*Pelargo'nium*-) leaf (Pl. I. fig. 1). These lines arise from the existence of passages between the cells, containing air; and they are called intercellular passages. By gently warming a section containing them in water over a spirit-lamp, or by moistening the section with a drop of spirit, the passages will be filled up with the liquid, so as to become transparent. When the intervals between the cells are larger and broader, they are called *intercellular spaces*.

So far, cells have been considered simply in regard

to their form, as vesicles, either rounded or altered in shape by mutual pressure. We have now to notice the matters contained within the cells, or the cell-contents.

Cell-contents. — In most cells, especially when young, a minute, rounded, colourless body may be seen, either in the middle or on one side, called the *nucleus*; this is very distinct in a cell of the pulp of an apple (Pl. I. fig. 2 *b*). And within this nucleus is often to be seen another smaller body, frequently appearing as a mere dot, called the *nucle'olus*.

The nucleus is imbedded in a soft substance, which fills up the entire cell (Pl. I. fig. 2 *c*); this is the pro'toplasm (πρῶτος, first, πλάσμα, formative substance). As it is very transparent, it is readily overlooked; but it may usually be shown distinctly by adding a little glycerine to the edge of the cover with a glass rod, when it contracts and separates from the cell-walls, as in the lower cell of fig. 2. The protoplasm in some cells is semisolid and of uniform consistence, while in others it is liquid in the centre, the outer portion being somewhat firmer and immediately in contact with the cell-wall. In the latter case, it forms an inner cell to the cell-wall, and is called the *primordial utricle*. The terms "protoplasm" and "primordial utricle" are, however, used by some authors synonymously.

The protoplasm is the essential part of the cell, and it forms or secretes the cell-wall upon its outer surface in the process of formation of the cell considered as a whole. It is also of different chemical composition from the cell-wall, being allied in this respect to animal matter.

Chlor'ophyll (χλωρὸς, green; φύλλον, leaf).—On examining a section of any green part of a plant, as the green substance of a Geranium- (*Pelargonium-*) leaf, it will be seen that the green colour does not arise from the whole substance being coloured, as appears to be the case to the naked eye, but from the presence of little grains or granules of a green colour-ing-matter in the protoplasm of the cells. This green matter is called chlorophyll. If the cells be crushed, the granules will escape, and can be examined in the separate state. Chlorophyll is most abundant in those parts of plants which are exposed to the light.

Starch.—In many cells of plants, particularly those which have attained their full growth, other granules, larger than those of chlorophyll, and colourless, are met with; these are the *starch-granules* (Pl. I. fig. 3). They are usually rounded or oblong, and exhibit on the surface a number of rings, one within the other, or concentric, as it is called. In the centre of the in-nermost ring is a black dot or streak, arising from the presence of a little pit or furrow, and called the *hilum*.

The starch-grains may be readily seen within cells in a thin section of a potato (Pl. I. fig. 4); here they are very numerous, and larger than in most other plants. A separate grain is represented in fig. 3.

The appearance of rings in the separate grains arises from the starch-granules being composed of numerous concentric coats or layers, like those of an onion.

A very simple and striking method of determining whether any granule is composed of starch or not, consists in adding to it, when placed in water on a slide, a drop of solution of iodine. As soon as this touches the granule, it assumes a beautiful purple colour, the depth of tint depending upon the quantity of the iodine-solution; if this be very considerable, the granule appears almost black. The section of potato forms a very interesting object when mois-tened with the iodine-solution, the starch-granules becoming beautifully coloured, whilst the cell-wall re-mains colourless, and the protoplasm becomes yellow.

The form of the starch-granules differs in different plants, so that the kind of plant from which starch has been derived may be distinguished by attention to the size, form, and structure of its starch-granules. Thus, the granules represented in Pl. I. fig. 3, which it will be noticed are all drawn under the same power, are derived from different plants,— *a* being those of wheat-flour, in which the hilum is obscure, and the rings faint; *b* is a granule of West Indian arrowroot, in which the hilum forms a transverse crack; *c* is a granule of potato-starch, in which the hilum is a dot, and the rings are very distinct; *d* represents the compound granules of the oat, the separate granules being figured below; *e* is a granule of lentil-starch, with its long dark hilum and elegant oval concentric rings; and *f* represents a compound and separate granule of rice-starch. It will be noticed that the granules of oat- and rice-starch are angular, as it is called.

The knowledge of the peculiar forms of the starch-granules is important in a practical point of view, for it enables us to recognize them when mixed as an adulteration with other substances, and also to distinguish the different kinds of starch from each other. Thus table-mustard, as it is called, is principally composed of the cheaper wheat- or pea-flour, which is easily recognized by the structure of the starch-grains. Arrowroot is considerably dearer than potato-starch; hence in trade the latter is fraudulently sold for the former, the adulteration being detected with difficulty by the eye, but easily under the microscope. Again, rice is largely mixed with wheat-flour, as it makes inferior flour into very white bread; and this may also be readily detected under the microscope. The reader can now understand how valuable the microscope is in detecting adulterations, with a knowledge of the various forms and structures of substances, especially with the aid of a few chemical tests.

Starch-grains are altered by boiling in water, becoming swollen and often changed into curious forms, the rings becoming faint or disappearing.   If a piece of boiled potato be examined, the starch-granules will seem to have vanished from the cells, which are swollen and covered with an irregular kind of network.   The network consists of parts of the protoplasm situated in the interstices of the starch-granules, and solidified or coagulated by the heat.   On crushing the cells by pressing upon the cover, the starch-granules will escape, swollen and partly fused together; but they may easily be recognized as consisting of starch by the iodine test.

The granules of " tous les mois " starch are particularly well adapted for showing the concentric rings, the granules being about twice as large as those of the potato.

Starch-granules are best examined in water; and a small quantity only of the starch must be placed on the slide, if the structure of the granules is to be seen clearly.   They may be mounted in glycerine, although this makes them very transparent.

To those who possess a polariscope, starch-granules are particularly interesting, as they exhibit a black cross, and, with a plate of selenite laid beneath the slide, a beautiful play of colours.

In addition to the starch and chlorophyll, the cells of plants contain other matters, as gum, sugar, &c.; but as they are dissolved in the cell-liquid, they are not visible.   In the cells of certain plants, however, spherical globules, with light centres and black outlines, will be met with : these consist of oil.

Raph'ides.—Lastly, occurring in the cells of plants, especially such as are soft and juicy (succulent), will be found minute, hard, colourless crystals, called *raphides* (ῥαφὶς, a needle).   These are most frequently needle-like or acicular (*acus*, a needle), but sometimes prismatic or rod-like with flat sides; they are also not unfrequently grouped into little tufts. They may be readily found in a piece of the stem of garden-rhubarb (Pl. I. fig. 5 *a*), or of the common balsam.

Porous and spiral cells.—The walls of the cells of cellular tissue are sometimes covered with little dots (Pl. I. fig. 11 *a*), or slit-like markings; the cells are then called porous cells. A specimen of them may be obtained from a section of the pith of the elder (*Sambúcus nígra*).

Sometimes cells exhibit the appearance of a spiral line marking their walls, as if a little bell-spring were coiled up in them (Pl. III. fig. 2 *a*). These are called spiral cells, or spiral fibrous cells, and the tissue formed by them is called fibro-cellular tissue.

We now leave the cells of ordinary cellular tissue, to examine those in which the dimension of length predominates, so that they form tubular cells; and first of those required to possess strength and firmness, combined with flexibility. These qualities are met with in the cells constituting

Woody tissue.—Of this there are two forms, called respectively wood-cells and woody fibres.

The *wood-cells* are moderately long, more or less tapering and overlapping at the ends; and the cell-walls are thickened, so as to possess considerable firmness. These cells are found in the wood of stems, as in the white woody portion of an ash stick, that of a lime-tree, the stem of a Chrysanthemum, &c. (Pl. I. fig. 6). They are closely packed, and the tissue formed by their union is called *prosen'chyma* (πρὸς, close, ἔγχυμα, tissue).

In the other kind of woody tissue the cells are very long and slender, strong, yet flexible, gradually tapering at the ends, where they overlap each other; and they have thick walls, so that, when divided transversely, the cavity appears almost filled up (Pl. I. figs. 5 *d*, 9, & 7 *b*). This tissue is called *woody fibre*

D

or *pleuren'chyma* (πλευρὰ, rib, ἔγχυμα), from its strength.

The walls of the cells of woody tissue are often covered with dots, either simple or with an inner dot (Pl. I. fig. 6 *b*, fig. 11 *b*), or with streaks (Pl. I. fig. 6 *a*) or with a spiral fibre (fig. 11 *b*, *c*), either alone or with dots also.

This tissue is of great importance in plants, from its strength and flexibility; it forms a considerable part of the veins of leaves, the inner bark (*liber*), and of the wood of the stems of trees. It is also very useful to man: for it constitutes hemp, of which rope and string are made; flax, of which linen is made; cocoa-nut fibre; bast, used by gardeners for tying up plants, which is the inner bark of the lime; and jute, which is the inner bark of an Indian lime-tree.

In the white woody part of the stems of trees belonging to the fir-order (Conif'eræ), as a piece of deal or pine, which is mainly composed of wood- (prosenchymatous) cells, the cells exhibit rows of minute circular markings (Pl. I. fig. 10). These were formerly supposed to be solid bodies or glands; hence the tissue is still sometimes called glandular. Within the outer ring of each marking is an inner central dot, or sometimes an oblique streak. The side view of the cells (Pl. I. fig. 8 *a*), which is seen in a tangential section, shows that the markings are minute pits, each being opposite to one of an adjacent cell, and sunk inwards towards the centre of the cell, the inner dot or streak being a thinner portion of the cell-wall. This glandular tissue of the Coniferæ is interesting as forming a test-object for the defining power of the microscope, which should show the two rings sharply and free from colour; the section of the wood should be examined as a dry transparent object.

The difference between the woody fibre and the wood-cells of coniferous wood may also be seen well in a piece of deal, as cut up for fire-wood. If the end of a stick of this be examined with the naked eye, parts of brown rings will be seen traversing the whiter portion of the wood. These brown rings consist of woody fibre; the white portion of wood-cells. On making a very thin transverse section, the interior of the woody fibres is seen to be almost entirely filled up (Pl. I. fig. 7 *b*), while the cavity of the wood-cells is much more open (Pl. I. fig. 7 *a*); the former also contain globules of turpentine.

It must be remarked here that some botanical authors include both forms of woody tissue under the term prosenchyma. But, as we shall see hereafter, the form of the prosenchymatous cells being sometimes used as a character for distinguishing the cells of leaves, to which the term pleurenchymatous cells would be inapplicable, the above distinction will be found important.

Vessels, vascular tissue.—In the next form of tubular cells, these are broader and softer than the cells of woody tissue, thin-walled, and the ends pointed; and their walls exhibit spiral or ring-like markings, or rows of dots (Pl. I. fig. 5 *c, e, b*), indicating the existence of one or more spiral fibres or rings. When the vessels contain spiral fibres, they are called spiral vessels (Pl. I. fig. 5 *c*); when they contain ring-shaped portions of fibre, they are called annular (*an'nulus*, a ring) vessels (Pl. I. fig. 5 *e*); and when the spaces between the fibres are partly filled up, leaving only dots, the deposit forming a kind of network, we have a reticulated (*réte*, a net) vessel (Pl. I. fig. 5 *b*). This tissue can easily be obtained from a piece of cooked rhubarb, the stem of a balsam, or from any soft-stemmed plant. Vessels very frequently contain air.

Ducts.—The tubular cells forming ducts (Pl. I. figs. 5 *b*, 11 *c*) are large, more or less flattened or blunt at the ends (truncated); and the cell-membrane at first closing the ends is often removed or absorbed, so that the ducts communicate with each other, to allow of the free passage of the sap through them. Their walls are invariably covered with markings, consisting of either simple or bordered dots, resembling those met with in the preceding forms of tissue. The ducts are often easily recognizable with the naked eye, in transverse sections of stems, by the large pores which they form in the wood. These may be well seen in a section of a piece of cane. The tissue composed of dotted ducts is called bothren'chyma (βόθρος, pit); but the term is principally applied to those ducts in which the dots are simple, i. e. have no inner dot.

The structure of the above forms of tissue may be best understood in relation to their development. It has been stated that the essential part of the cell is the protoplasm. As cells grow older, new matter is deposited by the protoplasm upon the inner surface of the cell-wall, either to a small extent, evenly and uniformly, as in ordinary parenchyma, or unevenly, in the form of spiral layers, forming fibres or bands, leaving bare spaces, where the original cell-wall exists alone. The matter thus deposited is called secondary deposit, the original cell-wall being the primary deposit. When the secondary deposit covers the interior of the cells except at certain slit-like spaces, we have the appearance figured in Pl. I. fig. 6 a). When the deposit forms a spiral fibre, or a series of rings, we have the spiral or annular vessel or duct. And when the interspaces between the coils of a close spiral fibre are filled up except at certain spots, we have the dotted or reticulated vessel or duct.

In many instances, these deposits are present together: thus, sometimes the outermost deposit leaves rounded pits or dots, while an inner portion forms a spiral fibre (Pl. I. fig. 11 b); or one layer leaves simple rounded pits, while the other leaves smaller slits or dots placed opposite the former (Pl. I. fig. 6 b).

In some cells the cavity is almost entirely filled up

by secondary deposit, which leaves minute canals radiating from a small cavity in the centre to the circumference, as seen in the transverse section of a plum-stone (Pl. I. fig. 56); here the canals appear as dark lines. In others, again, the secondary deposit forms several distinct layers, leaving channels very similar to those of the last; an example is met with in the gritty tissue of the pulp of a pear.

The obvious use of the pits and channels in the above tissues is to preserve the permeability of the walls of the elements, which would be destroyed if the walls were equally thickened all over.

Cell-formation.—New cells are formed by the division of old or parent cells. The actual process of division is difficult to observe, as it requires prolonged observation; but cells are often met with in all stages of division, of which some instances will be pointed out hereafter. The cell-division takes place in two ways, either according to the endogenous (ἔνδον, within, γεννάω, to produce), or the exogenous (ἔξω, outside, γεννάω) method. The manner in which the division takes place in the former is this:—At first a slight indentation or constriction of the protoplasm occurs at the line of division; this deepens until the protoplasm is completely divided. The freshly divided surfaces then become coated with a new portion of cell-wall, so as to make two or more new cells, which either remain in contact or separate from each other. In some cases, the divided portions of protoplasm become coated all over with new cell-walls.

In the exogenous process, a portion of the protoplasm protrudes from the surface of the cell, carrying the cell-wall before it, so as to form a little bud-like body; this is next cut off at its point of junction with the parent-cell, and coated, as in the first case, with a new cell-wall, so as to form a new cell.

Preparation.—In examining the vegetable elements and tissues, very thin sections must be made with a razor or thin sharp knife; these are then to be placed in a little water on a slide. As the structures are all minute, the distinctness with which they are seen will mainly depend upon the proper thinness of the sections. When sections of dry stems are to be examined, the black margins of the air-bubbles contained in the cells often render the structure indistinct; these must therefore be displaced by first wetting the tissue with methylated alcohol, and then adding water to it in a watch-glass or on a slide; or the tissue may be soaked in warm water for some hours: and this is mostly requisite in preparing thin sections of dry tissues.

Attention must also be paid to the manner in which the section is made, or the direction in which the portion of the plant is cut. There are three important directions which must be distinguished, producing transverse, longitudinal, and tangential sections. If the cuts be made across the length of a stem, for instance, the section is called transverse. If the cuts be made in the direction of the length, through the centre, the section is longitudinal; and if the cuts are made in a direction parallel to a line running down the centre of the stem, but nearer its margin, it is a tangential section. It is scarcely necessary to mention that an oblique section is intermediate between a transverse and a longitudinal section.

CHAPTER IV.

VEGETABLE ORGANS.

The vegetable elements and tissues which have been described form, either separately or by their combination in various ways, the organs of plants. To these we shall now pass, and consider the structure of the principal organs of the members of the vegetable kingdom.

Leaves.—Leaves in their simplest form consist of a single sheet or layer of parenchymatous cells or cellular tissue, an example of which may be found in almost any moss (Pl. III. fig. 30). The granules of chlorophyll will often be very distinctly seen in these cells. The first addition to this form of leaf is a row or two of prosenchymatous cells running longitudinally down the middle of the leaf, so as to form a rudimentary vein or nerve. In other and more highly developed leaves, the layers of cells are numerous, and traversed by bundles of wood-cells, vessels, and ducts (fibro-vascular tissue), forming the veins,— the entire surface being covered with a skin or membrane, called the epidermis.

Epider'mis (ἐπὶ, upon, δέρμα, skin).—This membrane is composed of one or more layers of colourless, closely packed cells (Pl. I. figs. 13 & 28), the colour it occasionally exhibits usually arising from some of the underlying cells of the leaf being seen through it, or remaining adherent to it when stripped from the leaf. It is easily separated, by making a cut in a soft leaf, and peeling it off with a fine pair of forceps, or by soaking a leaf for some time in water and then stripping it off. It must be remarked that the epidermis covers not only the leaves, but every part of the plant.

Hairs.—Arising from the epidermis are the hairs of plants. These are thread-like or filamentous pro-longations of the epidermis beyond the surface of the leaf (Pl. I. fig. 12), consisting of cells arranged end to end. They are often branched, sometimes star-shaped (stellate) (fig. 28), and present great varieties in form, as shown in the figures, the plants from which these were drawn being mentioned in the De-scription of the Plates. Sometimes hairs terminate in a little head (Pl. I. figs. 12 *c, d, e*), the cell or cells composing which secrete a colouring or a viscid sub-stance; they are then termed glandular. The hairs of plants are particularly interesting to the micro-scopic observer, not only on account of their curious forms, but in connexion with the remarkable pheno-menon of the circulation of the cell-contents, or *rotation*, as it is called, observable in them. This is difficult to be perceived by any one unaccustomed to microscopic observation, because the particles by which the motion of the cell-contents becomes evi-dent are exceedingly minute; but practice in the use of a high power will overcome this difficulty. The hairs which exhibit the phenomenon best are those of the American Spiderwort (*Tradescan'tia Virgin'ica*), which is to be found in every garden. It may, per-haps be recognized thus:—The plant is about a foot and a half high; the leaves are sword-shaped and channelled, and the flowers are purple, in heads, and 1½ inch in diameter. The hairs are attached to the sides of the stamens, towards the lower part or base. The stamens should be carefully picked off with for-ceps, and placed on a slide in a drop of water; the hairs should then be separated with the mounted needles, and a cover applied. Under a low power, the hairs are seen to be beaded or monil'iform (*moníle*, a necklace), and of a fine purple colour (Pl. I. fig. 22).

On applying a high power, as the $\frac{1}{4}$-inch, the individual cells will come distinctly into view, and the nucleus will be seen very clearly as a roundish granular mass (Pl. I. fig. 23 *a*). On carefully examining the cell-contents, delicate lines will be observed radiating irregularly from the nucleus, some passing to the top of the cells, while others run towards its base, as in the figure; and on very close inspection, the portions of protoplasm of which these lines consist, will be found to move slowly and steadily, the motion becoming perceptible by means of the minute granules of which the protoplasm consists. The currents return at the ends of the cell, there being no passage of the contents of one cell into the cavity of either of those adjacent. During this examination, it will be noticed that the surface of the cell-wall is striated with fine wrinkles.

It may be remarked that the hairs should be taken from flowers which have only just opened; for this curious and inexplicable rotation is connected with the growth of the cell; and when this has attained maturity, it no longer occurs. The phenomenon may be observed in many other hairs of plants, as those of common groundsel (*Senécio vulgáris*) (Pl. I. fig. 12 *a*, *b*), and in the cells of the leaves of some water-plants; but I must refer to the article "Rotation" in the Dictionary for further information.

The most important variety of hair is that derived from the Cotton-plant (a kind of Mallow), and forming the cotton of commerce. These hairs spring from the epidermis of the seeds. The cells composing it are very long and soft, becoming flaccid and easily bent when dry (Pl. IX. fig. 13).

Stings.—Stinging hairs or stings may be well illustrated by reference to the common large nettle (*Urtíca dioíca*). In this plant they consist of a thick-walled cell, bulbous at the base, which is imbedded in the epidermis (Pl. I. fig. 21), the pointed end being terminated by a very minute dilatation or knob. The sting contains an acrid liquid, which escapes when the little knob is broken off in wounding the skin, and produces the well-known irritation. By the side of the figure of the sting is represented the point of a fine needle (fig. 20), showing that the expression "sharp as a needle" has no force when microscopic bodies are in question.

Stom'ata (στόμα, mouth).—On viewing a strip of epidermis, the observer will be sure to notice certain oval or roundish bodies (Pl. I. fig. 13 *a*), composed of mostly two kidney-shaped cells in apposition but leaving a chink between them; these are the stomata. They communicate beneath with the intercellular passages, of which they may be considered the mouths; and by their agency a direct communication is established between these passages and the air. The two cells which guard the orifice are termed the "guard cells."

Stomata are most numerous on the under surface of leaves; they are entirely absent in plants growing under water, and in most of the lower plants. In many of the stomata, viewed in the ordinary way, the air situated between the guard cells is indicated by the black spot or dot present; but after a time, or by the application of a gentle heat to the slide, the air becomes displaced by the water, and their structure becomes very distinct.

In certain plants, the epidermis is imbued with flint or sil'ica; so that even when burnt to an ash the stomata are still quite distinct. Examples of this may be found in the stalk or culm of grasses, as in straw, the shining epidermis of which is siliceous; or the epidermis of canes. Among the lower plants, this peculiarity is especially curious in the species of *Equisétum*, or mares'-tails.

The manner in which the veins of leaves are arranged is worthy of special attention, as it forms one of the characters by which the two leading divisions of the Vegetable Kingdom are characterized. Thus in one of these divisions the veins are branched, so as to form a network throughout the leaf; the plants with these netted veins, to which belong our trees, shrubs, and most herbs, are the Dicotylédons, or Ex'ogens; while in the second division, the veins run parallel to each other, being little or not at all branched, and not forming a network. The plants with parallel veins, among which are our grasses, lilies, &c., are the Monocotylédons or En'dogens.

Stems.—In the stems of plants, the tissues are arranged round a centre; otherwise, in the simpler and lower plants, they agree in structure with leaves, the centre being occupied by some element of fibro-vascular tissue, as simple wood-cells, a few vessels or ducts.

In the higher or flowering plants, the stem exists in two distinct forms, corresponding to the differences above noticed in the arrangement of the veins of the leaves; these must be considered separately.

In the *Dicotyledons* or *Exogens* (Pl. I. fig. 36), the centre of the stem, in a transverse section, is seen to be occupied by the pith or *medulla*, which is represented in the figure by the innermost circle. Immediately outside and around this is a narrow ring, indicating the section of a sheath to the pith, and called the *medullary sheath*. Next comes a broad ring of wood of the first year's growth (fig. 36 *a*), traversed, from the pith to the bark, by wedge-shaped paler rays, termed the medullary rays. Outside the first year's wood is the newer and paler wood of the second year (*b*); and so on, a new ring of wood being added outside the preceding layer for each year of growth of the stem.

On the outer side of the wood is the inner bark or *liber* (fig. 36 *c*); and outside this is the spongy outer bark (*d*), covered by its epidermis.

These structures are of different composition, as may be best seen in longitudinal sections. The pith and the medullary rays consist of cellular tissue, the cells being mostly rounded in the former, and more closely pressed together and squarish in the latter. The medullary sheath consists of vascular tissue; and the wood, of wood-cells traversed longitudinally by bundles of vascular tissue and ducts, the latter being larger and more distinct towards its outer boundary. The liber is composed of woody fibre, and the outer bark of cellular tissue.

The new woody matter being deposited outside the old, between the bark and the previously formed layer, gives origin to the term exogen (ἔξω, outside, γεννάω, to produce). These structures may be examined in the section of a branch of the lime-tree or lilac.

In the *Monocotyledons* or *Endogens* (Pl. I. fig. 37), there is no distinct bark, nor pith, nor medullary rays—the entire stem consisting of cellular tissue with isolated bundles of fibro-vascular tissue scattered through it. Moreover the new substance is added to the centre of the stem, or within the old; hence the term endogen (ἔνδον, within, γεννάω). A section of a piece of cane will exhibit this structure.

To examine the structure of stems, sections must be made in various directions. The relative position of the component parts of a stem are best seen in a transverse section; but the structure of the tissues is most evident in longitudinal sections, and under the higher powers. The annual rings of the Exogens are best observed in transversely sawn-off pieces of perfectly dry stems, which have been polished with sand-paper, and varnished with spirit varnish.

Roots.—The structure of roots is very similar to that of stems; there is, however, no distinct pith, nor are there stomata on the epidermis; and the vessels are replaced by ducts. The very fine rootlets or radicles of water-plants often show the rotation of the protoplasm very distinctly.

Flowers.—The various parts of flowers, being each a modified leaf, present the same general structure as the latter. As the reader may not be acquainted with the names of these parts or organs in the higher plants, and as we shall have to compare them with their representatives in the lower forms of vegetable life, it will be well briefly to indicate them. A common and beautiful yet despised flower (Pl. I. fig. 32) may serve for illustration; this is chickweed (*Stellária média*), which can be found everywhere. The outermost circle of flower-leaves, which forms a kind of cup to the rest of the flower (*a*), is the *calyx*; the separate leaves being called the *sepals*. The row within this, in most flowers consisting of brilliantly coloured pieces, forms the *corolla* (*b*); the individual pieces being the *petals*. When the two kinds are equally coloured, or not distinguishable, the whole is called the *perianth*, as in a tulip. When the segments of the perianth are dry and chaffy, as in the flowers of grasses, the outermost are said to constitute the *glumes*, and the innermost the *paleæ*. Within the ring of petals are certain thread-like organs called *stamens* (*c*); and these consist of a *filament* (fig. 39 *a*), surmounted at the top or apex by the *anther* (fig. 39 *b*), which is usually coloured, and consists of two lobes. The anthers when ripe burst, and discharge a coloured dust; this is the *pollen*. Lastly, within the stamens is the central organ of the flower, the *pistil*, and sometimes there are several of them. The pistil consists of three parts, viz. a swollen base, the *ovary* (fig. 41 *b*), surmounted by a column or *style* (fig. 41 *a*), and which is crowned by a viscid and often hairy summit, the *stigma* (fig. 40*). In chickweed there are 3 styles.

It must be remarked that, in the flowers of some plants, stamens alone are present, while others con-

E

tain pistils only, although most flowers contain both organs. When the stamens and pistils occur in separate flowers on the same plant, the plant is said to be *monœcious* (μόνος, single, οἶκος, family); when all the flowers of distinct plants contain either stamens only or pistils only, the plant is *diœcious* (δὶς, twice, οἶκος); and when the stamens and pistils occur together in all the flowers of the same plant, the plant is said to be *hermaphrodite*. These terms had their origin in the idea that the differences of plants in respect to these organs were analogous to those of the sexes in animals. All the parts of a flower have their special uses: thus the calyx and corolla protect the delicate organs enclosed by them, until they attain maturity. The petals also, by their brilliant colours, attract insects which feed upon or collect the honey of the flowers; these at the same time conveying the pollen which adheres to their bodies from one flower to the stigma of another. The stamens and pistils are organs of fructification, it being essential for the fertilization of the flowers that the pollen should come into contact with the stigma. We will now consider some interesting points of structure in these organs.

Petals.—The petals often form most beautiful microscopic objects, on account of the curious shape and structure of the cells of their epidermis, and the splendid tints of the colouring matters contained in them. As petals are mostly too thick to allow of the cells being distinctly seen in the entire state, a little cut should be made in them while gently stretched on the finger, and the epidermis carefully stripped off with forceps; the strip should then be laid on the slide in water as usual: in this way the curious patterns of the epidermic cells will become very distinct. The petals of a red geranium (*Pelargónium*) may be used to illustrate them (Pl. I. fig. 24). The structure may be best understood by reference to the epidermis of the leaf of a geranium (Pl. I. fig. 13),

in which the cells present wavy or undulate walls.
In the petal (fig. 24), the walls are inflexed at tolerably regular distances, so as to give rise to the appearance of a row of teeth lining the cell. If the
strip of petal be folded, so as to exhibit the side view,
it will also be seen that the cells project outwards
from the surface to form a bluntish point or papilla,
or the petals are papillose as it is called; and the
surface of the membrane around the papillæ is finely
wrinkled, so as to present the appearance of very delicate radiating lines or striæ. Intermediate degrees
of this inflexion may be found in various flowers,
between the slight condition seen in fig. 13 and the
extreme state of fig. 24, as in the snapdragon (*An-
tirrhinum május*).

Anthers.—The cavities of the anthers are lined
with fibro-cellular tissue, the fibres of which aid in
discharging the pollen; this may be seen by dissecting an anther of London pride (*Saxifraga umbrósa*),
or of a wallflower (*Cheiran'thus cheíri*) in water. It
also exists in chickweed.

Pollen.—The pollen consists of minute grains called
the *pollen-granules.* They may be viewed either in
the dry state as opake objects, or when immersed in
water as transparent objects. As it is often difficult
to moisten them, they may be touched on the slide
with a little spirit, and then a drop of water added.
Their forms are very varied and curious, but they are
difficult of observation from their minute size. They
consist of one or more coloured cells, and these cells
are remarkable for their surfaces exhibiting spines,
networks, folds, and markings of various kinds. Thus
in the primrose the pollen-granules are cylindrical,
the surface being furrowed (Pl. I. fig. 16); in the sunflower the granules are spherical, and covered with
tubercles surmounted by spines (fig. 17); in the
garden convolvulus the surface of the spherical granules is covered with an elegant network, in the

meshes of which are also situated spines (fig. 18) ; and in the granules of chickweed the surface presents pits, with minute tubercles in the centre (figs. 30 & 31). The pollen-granules are often considerably altered by immersion in water; so that, in judging of their structure when examined in water, the resulting alteration must be taken into account.

When ripe pollen-granules have been immersed in water for a short time, one or more minute tubes will be seen protruding from their surface; these are the *pollen-tubes,* and the granular protoplasm contained in them is called the *fovil'la.* In the process of fertilization of the flower, the pollen-granules fall upon the viscid stigma; the pollen-tubes are then protruded, and, passing down the intercellular spaces of the style (Pl. I. fig. 14), enter an aperture in the ovule or young seed, which is thus endowed with the power of growing into a new plant. The pollen-tubes are often very long, and they do not exist fully developed in the pollen-granules, but grow down the style, just as the little rootlet of a seed grows into the soil. The style of a crocus will serve for dissecting out with mounted needles the long and very slender pollen-tube (Pl. I. fig. 15).

O'vary.—The ovary by its growth and enlargement becomes the fruit. There are many interesting microscopic structures to be found in fruits and the seeds they contain, a few of which may be noticed here.

On examining the surface of the rind or pericarp (περὶ, around, καρπὸς, fruit) of an orange, little dots will be seen, paler than the rest of the surface. These are receptacles of secretion, or glands, containing the evaporable or volatile oil upon which the fragrance of the orange depends. They consist of loose cells, surrounding a central cavity, and are imbedded in the rind.

Other receptacles of secretion, called *vittæ* (*vitta*, a band), occur in the wall (pericarp) of the fruit of the Umbelliferæ, or Parsley Order of plants, and their arrangement forms characters for distinguishing the genera. They may be well seen in caraway-seeds; for the caraway-plant is one of the Umbelliferæ. It must be observed that a caraway "seed" is not really a seed, but consists of half the fruit; for, on careful examination, one side of it will be found to be flattened, the flattening resulting from the mutual pressure of the two half-fruits at that part; moreover the dried style exists at its summit. In the figure (Pl. I. fig. 19), the flattened part of the seed is next the observer. The seed has five evident longitudinal ridges, one at each corner or angle. The vittæ are dark-coloured (fig. 19 *a*), and placed one between each pair of these ridges; and they consist of long flattened spaces in the substance of the pericarp, with transverse markings, indicating internal cross partitions, In botanical works, the presence of five ridges, with single vittæ in the intervals, is given as a character by which the half-fruits (carpels) of the caraway are to be distinguished. But on closely inspecting the flattened surface, another ridge is seen running down its middle; so that the seed really has six ridges, one of which is smaller than the rest from the pressure of the other half. Hence the character of five ridges with single vittæ is incorrect.

The vittæ contain the volatile oil to which the fragrance and pungency of the fruit is owing, although some of the oil exists also in the cells of the kernel or albúmen, which forms the white and greater part of the seed.

The skin of a reddish apple, peeled off in the manner described for petals, exhibits beautifully the red colouring matter of different tints in adjacent cells, while the pulp displays the cell-contents, as already mentioned. The latter may also be easily examined, from their large size, in most of the softer fruits, as that of the snowberry or the cucumber.

As the ovary or fruit approaches maturity, the petals and stamens wither and fall off, the calyx often remaining, and being sometimes adherent to the ovary, at others free or unattached to it.

Seeds.—During the ripening of the fruit, the seeds contained within it are gradually becoming further developed.

The seeds themselves are covered outside by a skin or coat called the *testa* (*testa*, a shell). This is remarkable for frequently displaying various kinds of figured patterns, consisting of raised networks, ridges, little knobs or tubercles, &c. Examples of these may be found in the seeds of the poppy (Pl. I. fig. 27), mignonette (fig. 29), and chickweed (fig. 51).

Some seeds are winged, as it is called, *i. e.* furnished with an extension of the testa beyond the margin of the seed. This not unfrequently consists of aggregated fibre-cells, the spiral fibre being very distinct, as in the seeds of *Eccremocar'pus scáber* (Pl. I. fig. 52). In the seeds of another curious plant in this respect, viz. *Collómia grandiflóra*, the fibre-cells are separate, so as to resemble hairs, and very mucilaginous, and in the dry seed are closely pressed to its surface. If a portion of the testa of these seeds, which can be procured at the seed-shops, be cut off, laid on a slide, a cover applied, and when the object is in focus, a drop of water be added, in a short time water softens the mucilaginous walls of the cells, the power of the spiral fibres comes into play, and the cells expand so as to form a very interesting object; the cells, in their expansion, apparently writhing like so many minute worms (Pl. I. fig. 35).

The seed itself, which is contained within the testa or seed-coat, consists essentially of the young plant or embryo. This is composed of three parts, viz. the *plúmule* (*plumula*, a little feather), or the young stem;

the *rad'icle* (*radicula*, a little root), or the young root; and one or two, rarely more, imperfectly developed or rudimentary leaves, the *cotyle'dons* (κοτυληδὼν, a cup).

These structures are closely packed in the seed, and are not easily recognized at first. By keeping seeds moist for a day or two until they begin to grow, or *germinate* as the seed-growth is called, they are readily detected, and may then be more easily found in the dry seed.

When somewhat advanced in growth, they are familiar to every one, although they may not be recognized by their names. In table "mustard and cress," the whole consists of these organs of the two plants; the white stalk directed downwards being the radicle, the two green leaf-like lobes the cotyledons, and between the latter directed upwards is the very minute plumule, which is more easily seen when the plants have been allowed to grow larger. This structure of the seed is important to be known, because the absence or presence and the number of cotyledons afford characters, corresponding with those already mentioned in respect to the veins of the leaves and the structure of the stem, for distinguishing the great divisions of the Vegetable Kingdom. Thus, the Exogens are Dicotyledons (δὶς, twice), their seeds having two cotyledons; while the Endogens are Monocotyledons (μόνος, single), having one only; and the Cryptogam'ic plants are Acotyledons (α, without), their seeds (spores) having none of these organs.

Some seeds consist entirely of the embryo, surrounded by the testa. But in many others there is also present a usually whitish, firm cellular substance, called the *albúmen* (*albumen*, white of egg).

The albumen of seeds often affords good specimens of secondary deposit, the cells being almost entirely filled with it. An example may be found in a section of vegetable ivory, of which ornaments are sometimes made; its structure resembles essentially that of the plum-stone. In other instances the cells contain secreted matters, as starch, oil, &c.; and sometimes the cotyledons also contain starch and oil. An example of the former exists in the albumen of wheat; and of the latter, in the horse-chestnut, the filbert, and mustard-seed.

The albumen and cotyledons serve to supply the embryo with nutriment until the roots have grown sufficiently to enable them to absorb it from the soil; the cotyledons also serve as temporary leaves.

The form and relative position of the radicle and cotyledons serve to distinguish certain groups of plants. This may be illustrated by the natural order Cruciferæ, or that containing the mustard, wall-flower, &c.

Thus, in one group, which may be represented by the wall-flower, the cotyledons are flat or plane (Pl. I. figs. 43 & 44), the radicle being applied to their edges. This is best seen in a transverse section (fig. 43). They are then called *accum'bent* (*accumbo*, to lie against); and the botanical sign is 0=. In the second group, the cotyledons are plane (Pl. I. fig. 38), with the radicle applied to the back of one of them, as in the seed of the common shepherd's purse (*Capsel'la bur'sa pastóris*) (Pl. VII. fig. 19). They are then termed *in'cumbent* (*incumbo*, to lie upon), and the sign is 0||. While in the third group the cotyledons are folded in the middle, like the leaves of a book (Pl. I. figs. 49 & 50), and the radicle is enclosed between them, as in the white mustard (*Sina'pis alba*). The cotyledons are then called *condu'plicate* (*conduplico*, to fold); and their sign is 0> >.

The plants above-mentioned are evidently all Dicotyledonous, or their seeds have two cotyledons; and they contain no albumen.

In the Monocotyledonous division, which may be represented by a grain of wheat (Pl. I. fig. 53), the

single cotyledon forms a minute sheath (*a*), enclosing
the plumule (*b*), the radicle (*c*) being here but little
developed at first, the greater part of the grain consisting of the albumen (*d*); the grain should be softened in water before examination. In the germi-
nated grain the cotyledon appears as a pale sheath,
surrounding the convolute green leaves of the plumule; which may be best seen in a transverse section
(Pl. I. fig. 48).

Fertilization.—A few words must now be said
regarding the formation of seeds, and the action of
the pollen-tubes in the process of fertilization.

In the earliest stages of growth, the young seeds,
or *ovules* as they are called, appear as little buds,
arising from the inner wall of the ovary; and the
part from which they arise is called the *placen'ta*
(*placenta*, a cake). In chickweed (Pl. I. fig. 41 *c*),
the placenta forms a central column; and when the
ovules are a little older, they are found to have separated somewhat from the placenta, but retaining a
connexion by means of a little cord or stalk, termed
the *funic'ulus* (*funis*, a cord). The ovules may be
readily found in the ovary or young pod of a wallflower, the placentas forming four lines, running longitudinally down the interior of the pod.

In this early condition the ovule consists of a mass
of cellular tissue; and as new formations are soon
added to it, it is termed in this state the *núcleus*.
Around the nucleus are then formed two coats, an
outer, called the *príminc*, and an inner, termed the se-
cun'dine. These coats or membranes are open at one
end, so as to leave a passage down to the apex of the
nucleus; the opening is called the *forámen*. These
structures are well seen in the ovule of the wallflower
(Pl. I. fig. 54), the foramen in the figure being indicated by a *; it will be noticed also that the funiculus runs down one side of the ovule, so as to terminate at the bottom or base of the nucleus. In

ripe seeds, the spot at which the funiculus has been attached is mostly perceptible in the form of a scar. The slight prominence of the foramen can also often be distinguished, as in the seed of chickweed (Pl. I. fig. 51*); in the ripe seed the foramen is termed the *micropyle,* and towards it the radicle of the embryo is always directed.

One of the cells of the nucleus near its apex then enlarges, so as to form a sac, called the *embryo-sac.* This is excessively thin and transparent (Pl. I. figs. 45 *b* & 47); and in it, also at the end next the foramen, one or more (in the chickweed one) smaller cells are formed from the cell-contents of the embryo-sac, which are called the *embryonal vesicles* (Pl. I. fig. 45 *a*).

Thus far developed, the embryo exists prior to the expansion of the flower and the discharge of the pollen. The embryo-sac is not figured in this early condition, the embryonal vesicle being then smaller than that in fig. 45 *b,* although occupying the same position.

When the pollen has escaped from the anthers and fallen upon the stigma, the pollen-tubes growing down the intercellular passages of the style, enter the foramen of the ovule, and so reach the apex of the nucleus, at which the embryonal vesicle contained in the embryo-sac is situated. The end of the pollen-tube then adheres to the embryonal vesicle, and such interchange of cell-contents takes place between them as effects fertilization.

The process of cell-formation in the fertilized embryonal vesicle then takes place rapidly, new cells being formed by the division of its cell-contents (Pl. I. fig. 45 *a*); and it will be noticed that the new cells are formed at the end of the embryonal vesicle, opposite to that situated at the apex of the embryo-sac. As the cell-division and formation proceed further, a mass of new cells is produced (Pl. I. figs. 46 *c*

& 47), forming the rudimentary embryo; and from
this, by further growth, the perfected embryo (fig. 55)
results; or, to use a fashionable technical term, the
simply cellular embryonic mass becomes differen-
tiated into the radicle, cotyledons, and plumule, forming the embryo. It will be remarked that the position of the embryo in fig. 55 is the reverse of that in
figs. 46 & 47, the radicle in the former being directed
downwards, whilst that of the embryo in the figure of
the embryo-sac (fig. 47) is directed upwards.

The embryonal structures are very difficult of detection; but it happens that in our little chickweed
they are more easily dissected out than in most other
plants. For this purpose, the ovules, placed on a
slide and lying in water, should be picked to pieces
with the mounted needles, under the simple microscope. They may be preserved in chloride of calcium
or glycerine.

A clear distinction must be drawn between seeds,
which result from the process of fertilization, and
buds, which are formed independently of this process.
Both consist essentially of embryo plants; but while
the former originate from a single cell, the latter are
outgrowths of a parent stem, from which their tissues
are derived; and while the former propagate the species, the latter increase the individual.

The obvious use of seeds is the distribution of the
species by the formation of new individuals.

In the general outline which has been given of the
elements, tissues, and organs of plants, they have
been examined principally as existing in the higher
groups, or those of more complex structure; and to
enter further upon a description of these plants would
involve the consideration of variations in the form
and arrangement of the organs of which they are
composed. As these can mostly be investigated without the use of the microscope, we must pass to those
in which the entire plant consists of little more than

simple or parenchymatous cells, and in which the representatives of the flower are so inconspicuous, or are reduced to so elementary a condition, that the plants included in the Division have been termed *Cryptogam'ic* (κρυπτὸς, concealed, γάμος, union—figuratively for reproductive organs) or Flowerless Plants. The reproductive organs of the Cryptogamia are usually termed the fructification, implying that they produce fruit, but not flowers.

PLATE II.   [PAGE 49.]

FERNS AND LICHENS.

Fig.
1. *Chlorococcum vulgare.*
2. *Parmelia parietina.*
3. *Parmelia parietina,* section of a saucer (apothecium).
4. *Parmelia parietina,* gonidia and asci.
5. *Parmelia parietina,* asci and paraphyses; 5 *a,* spores.
6. *Calicium clavellum.*
7. *Calicium clavellum,* stalked apothecia.
8. *Calicium clavellum,* apothecium.
9. *Polypodium vulgare,* frond.
10. *Polypodium vulgare,* lobe of frond.
11. *Polypodium vulgare,* group of capsules (thecæ).
12. *Polypodium vulgare,* capsule and spores.
13. *Polypodium vulgare,* spore germinating.
14. *Polypodium vulgare,* prothallium.
15. *Polypodium vulgare,* portion of prothallium, with archegonia.

Fig.
16. *Aspidium filix mas,* frond.
17. *Aspidium filix mas,* pinnules with sori.
18. *Aspidium filix mas,* single pinnule.
19. *Scolopendrium vulgare,* frond.
20. *Scolopendrium vulgare,* portion of frond.
21. *Cladonia coccifera.*
22. *Cladonia cornuta.*
23. *Cladonia pyxidata.*
24. *Cladonia rangiferina.*
25. *Cladonia rangiferina,* ends of podetium.
26. *Graphis scripta.*
27. *Graphis scripta,* lirellæ.
28. *Graphis scripta,* asci and spores.
29. *Graphis scripta,* spore.
30. *Opegrapha betulina.*
31. *Opegrapha betulina,* lirellæ.
32. *Opegrapha betulina,* lirella.
33. *Opegrapha betulina,* ascus with spores.
34. Scalariform ducts of Brake (*Pteris*).

Plate II.

CHAPTER V.

FERNS, OR FIL'ICES.

THE general appearance of plants belonging to the class of Ferns is so well known that it need scarcely be described, especially since the introduction of the glass plant-cases, by means of which the air can be kept so damp that ferns are now grown in the very heart of our cities. Their bright green and finely cleft leaves (Pl. II. figs. 9 & 16) or fronds (*frons*, a leaf) as the leaf-like organs of the lower plants are called, arising in tufts from the stems, give them the elegant appearance we are called upon to admire, whenever they are met with. The brownish spots or stripes seen upon the back or under surface of the fronds, and consisting of the fructification, form also a simple character by which they may generally be distinguished; although in a few of them the fructification is placed upon a distinct stalk. The stem or rhi'zome (ῥίζωμα, a root) of a fern is mostly situated just beneath or at the surface of the ground, and is commonly mistaken for the real root, which is buried in the earth. It is brownish outside, and covered with scurfy scales or *ramen'ta* (*ramentum*, a shaving). These scales are interesting microscopic objects, from the distinctness with which they exhibit the cellular network.

A section of the rhizome exhibits the fibro-vascular tissue arranged differently from that in the stems of either Exogens or Endogens. It forms curiously curved longitudinal plates, a very abundant component of which is the scalar'iform (*scala*, a ladder) duct (Pl. II. fig. 34). The walls of the scalariform ducts are angular, and the secondary deposit is ar-

F

ranged in the form of transverse bars, somewhat resembling the steps of a ladder ; which structure is best seen in a transverse or slightly oblique section. The fronds are usually cleft nearly down to the main vein or midrib (fig. 9), or pinnatifíd (*pinna*, a feather, *findo*, to cleave); sometimes the segments are similarly cleft, so that the fronds are bipinnatifid. The manner in which the veins usually branch is also peculiar, each branch separating from the point of division at an acute angle with the original direction of the vein (fig. 20), so as to be forked. It is also worthy of notice, that the young frond is rolled up into a flat spiral, or is cir′cinate (*circino*, to go round), before it opens.

We will now examine one or two species more minutely.

POLYPODIACEÆ. *Polypódium vulga′re* (Pl. II. fig. 9, one-third of the natural size), a member of this family, is very common on old trunks of trees, on banks, &c. The frond is deeply pinnatifid, the segments being oblong, blunt (obtuse), scalloped (crenate) at the edges (Pl. II. fig. 10), and becoming gradually shorter towards the apex of the frond.

On the back of the fronds are the little orange-coloured groups of capsules (Pl. II. figs. 9 & 10); these are called *sor′i* (σωρὸς, a heap). The capsules or *thécæ* (θήκη, a case), a magnified group of which is represented in fig. 11, consist each of an aggregation of cells, fixed to a stalk (fig. 12) ; and along the back of the capsule is a close row of thicker cells, forming an elastic ring, the *an′nulus*. When the seed-like bodies or spores (σπορὰ, a seed) are ripe, the annulus becomes straightened from its elastic power, and tears the capsule open, so that the spores are set free and scattered.

Aspid′ium filix mas (Pl. II. fig. 16, reduced to one third or fourth of the natural size), is the most common British fern. In this the fronds are pinnate, *i. e.* the segments (pinnæ) corresponding to those of *Polypo-dium* are cleft entirely to the main stalk, the pinnæ (fig. 17) being pinnatifid; and the segments of the pinnæ or the pinnules (fig. 18) are oblong, obtuse, and saw-edged (serrate). In all botanical works the fronds are incorrectly said to be bipinnate.

The sori are brown, kidney-shaped (fig. 18), and differ from those of *Polypodium* in being covered by a thin membrane (*indúsium*), which is fixed to the frond at the notch.

Scolopen'drium vulgáre (Pl. II. fig. 19), the Hart's-tongue Fern, is common in hedges and on moist banks. Its fronds are simple or undivided, strap-shaped, heart-shaped at the base, and narrowed to a point at the apex. The sori (fig. 20) are brown, narrow, longish (linear), and transverse or slightly oblique. The indusium is cleft down the middle, so as to form a longitudinal fissure or suture.

Reproduction.—The spores of the ferns (Pl. II. fig. 12 *a*) resemble in appearance the seeds of flowering plants on a small scale. They are usually brown, covered on the surface with little tubercles or other markings, and when kept on a slide in a moist atmosphere, as over a saucer of water covered with a bell-glass, they germinate. When this takes place, one or more short, brownish, hair-like radicles emerge from one part of the surface (Pl. II. fig. 13), and a process containing chlorophyll issues from an adjacent spot. As growth proceeds, the latter by cell-division gives rise to a flattened two-lobed leafy cotyledon-like body or *prothal'lium* (πρὸ, before, θαλλὸς, leaf), with nume-rous rootlets springing from the base of the lobes. The prothallium is of a peculiar dull-green colour, different from that of the young frond which is subse-quently formed. This arises from the absence of stomata and intercellular passages containing air; for the air in these passages of leaves and petals contri-butes greatly to the production of the brightness of their colours. Moreover, the cells of the prothallium resemble those of the parenchyma of a leaf, the epidermis with its wavy-margined cells being absent.

When the prothallium has attained its full development, minute scattered protrusions from its cells occur on the margin or under surface, resembling short and blunt hairs; and each of these becomes partitioned off to form a new cell, within which a number of crowded smaller cells are produced. These organs are called *antherid'ia* (anther, and εἶδος, resemblance); and within each of the crowded smaller cells is contained a very minute, colourless, coiled fibre, furnished with still finer filaments, called *cil'ia* (*cilium*, an eyelash); the ciliated fibres being termed *spermatozo'a* (σπέρμα, seed, ζῷον, animal). At a later period, other organs are found also on the back of the prothallium. These are larger than the antheridia, and are composed of several cells, arranged around a central canal which leads to an embryo-cell situated at its base (Pl. II. fig. 2). These organs are the *archegónia* (ἀρχή, beginning, γόνος, offspring). When the antheridia are ripe, they discharge the spermatozoa, which are enabled to swim about by means of their cilia in water (rain), and entering the canal, reach the embryo-cell, which thus becomes fertilized. When fertilized, the embryo-cells produce the little fronds which afterwards grow into the mature plants.

Hence the spores of ferns differ strikingly from the seeds of the higher plants in not containing the embryo radicle and cotyledons already formed, these being produced during or after germination; also in the fertilizing organs, viz. the antheridia or representatives of the anthers, and the archegonia or the representatives of the pistils, being produced from the cells of the prothallium.

The more minute of these structures are too difficult of observation and preparation for any one unaccustomed to microscopic manipulation, so that they have not been figured in detail; the figures given will, however, serve to guide the observer in their recognition.

Preservation.—The ferns may be easily preserved in the entire state, by laying them flat between sheets of coarse unsized paper, and subjecting them to moderate pressure in a screw-press; the paper should be changed, or dried before a fire every two or three days, and the pressure repeated until the specimens become dry and rigid. They may then be mounted on sheets of paper, being fastened either with thread passed round the stalk or portions of the frond with a needle, and tied in a knot behind, or with strips of paper gummed at the ends.

The minute structures may be preserved either in the dry state or in glycerine.

CHAPTER VI.

MOSSES, OR MUS'CI (MUSCUS, MOSS).

I NEED scarcely refer to the figures in Pl. III. to enable the reader to recognize the Mosses; every one knows them at once by their remarkably uniform general appearance, their miniature-plantlike form, their crowded little leaves, concealing the slender wiry stems, their growth in patches, and their curious urn-shaped fruits raised up on slender bristle-like stalks.

The leaves of the mosses are simple, *i. e.* not cut into segments, and consist of one or two layers of cells. The thinness of the leaves enables these cells to be seen very distinctly, the closely united cell-walls giving the leaves a netted or reticulated appearance (fig. 48), and the grains of chlorophyll being generally few and readily distinguished. The veins of the leaves, or the nerves as they are usually called, scarcely deserve the name; for neither they nor even the stems contain fibro-vascular tissue, but consist simply of elongate closely packed cells, and often the leaves have no nerves.

The fruit of the mosses consists of a *capsule,* sometimes called a *sporan'gium* (σπορὰ, seed, ἄγγος, vessel), usually placed at the end of a slender stalk, called the *séta* (*seta,* a bristle); but sometimes the stalk is absent or extremely short, when the capsule is said to be ses'sile (*sessilis,* sitting). The young capsule is covered with a thin extinguisher-like cap or *calyp'tra* (καλύπτρα, a cover), which is carried up as the capsule and its stalk grow, so as to be either entirely thrown off, or to remain covering a greater or less portion of the capsule, when this attains maturity.

PLATE III. [PAGE 54.]

MOSSES.

Fig.
1. *Sphagnum acutifolium*, expanded leaf.
2. *Sphagnum acutifolium*, cells of leaf.
3. Spermatozoa of *Polytrichum piliferum*.
4. *Sphagnum acutifolium*.
5. *Sphagnum acutifolium*, capsule.
6. *Gymnostomum truncatulum*.
7. *Gymnostomum truncatulum*, leaf.
8. *Gymnostomum truncatulum*, capsule and operculum.
9. *Gymnostomum truncatulum*, spore.
10. *Dicranum heteromallum*.
11. *Dicranum heteromallum*.
12. *Dicranum heteromallum*, leaf.
13. *Dicranum heteromallum*, operculum.
14. *Dicranum heteromallum*, calyptra.
15. *Dicranum heteromallum*, capsule; 15 *a*, peristome.
16. *Tortula muralis*.
17. *Tortula muralis*, leaf.
18. *Tortula muralis*, capsule : *a*, tooth of peristome.
19. *Tortula muralis*, operculum.
20. *Tortula muralis*, calyptra.
21. *Tortula muralis*, archegonia.
22. *Polytrichum piliferum*.
23. *Polytrichum piliferum*, leaf.
24. *Polytrichum piliferum*, calyptra.
25. *Polytrichum piliferum*, antheridial stems.

Fig.
26. *Polytrichum piliferum*, single head.
27. *Polytrichum piliferum*, antheridia and paraphyses.
28. *Funaria hygrometrica*.
29. *Funaria hygrometrica*.
30. *Funaria hygrometrica*, leaf.
31. *Funaria hygrometrica*, capsule; *a*, operculum.
32. *Funaria hygrometrica*, stalk-like body.
33. *Funaria hygrometrica*, young archegone.
34. *Funaria hygrometrica*, more advanced archegone.
35. *Funaria hygrometrica*, section of young capsule.
36. *Funaria hygrometrica*, calyptra.
37. *Funaria hygrometrica*, antheridia.
38. *Funaria hygrometrica*, spores.
39. *Funaria hygrometrica*, annulus.
40. *Funaria hygrometrica*, archegonia.
41. *Funaria hygrometrica*, antheridial head.
42. *Funaria hygrometrica*, peristome.
43. *Hypnum rutabulum*.
44. *Hypnum rutabulum*, leaf.
45. *Hypnum rutabulum*, capsule.
46. *Hypnum rutabulum*, spores.
47. *Hypnum rutabulum*, peristome.
48. *Hypnum rutabulum*, cells of leaf.
49. *Bryum capillare*.

The calyptra is either simply mitre-shaped, or *mitri-form* (Pl. III. fig. 24), or it is half-cleft, or *dimid'iate* (figs. 14, 36). When the capsule is ripe, the upper part usually separates at a circular horizontal line (fig. 8) as a kind of lid, which is called the *oper'-culum* (*operculum*, a lid), and thus the spores are enabled to escape. The rim of the capsule, from which the operculum has separated, forms its mouth, and this often exhibits a fringe of teeth (figs. 15, 18, 31), arranged in one or more rows; sometimes the teeth are replaced by a membrane, or, again, both teeth and a membrane may be present. This mouth-fringe is the *per'istome* (περὶ, around, στόμα, mouth). In many mosses, an elastic row or ring of cells is situated between the mouth of the capsule and its operculum, called the *annulus* (figs. 18 & 39); this, when the capsule is ripe, aids in throwing off the operculum.

It is important to become acquainted with the structure and arrangement of these parts, as they form characters by which the families and genera of mosses are distinguished.

The capsules of the mosses form very beautiful microscopic objects, especially those furnished with a toothed peristome.

Most of the mosses produce their fructification in the winter and spring.

The class of mosses is divided into two Orders, according to whether the fruit-stalk is terminal, *i. e.* arises from the end of the stem or its branches, or whether it is lateral, arising from the side of the stem. Those with the fruit-stalk terminal, or the end fruited (Pl. III. fig. 22), form the *Ac'rocarpi* (ἄκρα, summit, καρπὸς, fruit); while those with the fruit-stalks lateral, or the side-fruited mosses (fig. 43), constitute the *Pleu'rocarpi* (πλευρὰ, side). The new shoots or young branches of the stems of mosses are termed *innovations*.

We will now examine a few common mosses more
in detail, beginning with the ACROCARPI.

Sphag'num acutifólium (Pl. III. fig. 4) is found in
pools or bogs, growing at the margins so as to be
partially immersed. In this moss, the upper branches
are grouped into a head. The leaves are crowded,
and overlapping or im'bricate (*imbrex*, a tile) on the
elongate stems; they are egg-shaped (ovate) on the
main stems (fig. 1), and narrower or ovate-lanceolate
on the branches; they are nerveless, and finely
toothed at the apex. The capsule (fig. 5) is roundish-
ovate, without a peristome, and the operculum is
flattened. The grouped arrangement of the upper
branches renders the species of *Sphagnum* easily recognized. The structure of the leaves is also very
peculiar and characteristic (fig. 2). The cells of which
they consist are of two kinds, one (fig. 2 *a*) being
colourless, elongate, pointed, and containing a spiral
fibre; the other consisting of shorter and narrower
obtuse cells, containing chlorophyll, and situated between the former. In many of the former kind of
cells, little round apertures exist on the under surface,
and minute animals may sometimes be found im-
prisoned in them.

Another species of *Sphagnum*, *S. obtusifolium*, is
common, and greatly resembles the above, but has
shorter and thicker stems, and rounded-ovate, very
concave, and obtuse leaves.

Gymnos'tomum truncat'ulum (Pl. III. fig. 6) is a
common little moss, found on banks and in fields
and gardens.

In this there is no peristome, although, in the
young condition, a membrane extends more or less
over the interior of the mouth of the capsule. The
stem is slender, rigid, and simple, or but little
branched. The calyptra is dimidiate; the operculum
is present (fig. 8), and terminates above in an oblique
beak, or it is obliquely rostrate (*ros'trum*, a beak) as

it is called. The leaves are obovate (fig. 7) or ovate with the broader part remote from the stem, and narrowed at the apex, where the nerve protrudes or is ex'current (*excurro*, to run out). The spores (fig. 9) are reddish brown and smooth.

Dicránum heteromal'lum (Pl. III. figs. 10 & 11) is probably the first moss the reader will meet with on banks and heaths in the early spring; and it will be sure to be noticed on account of the bright green colour of the patches and the beautiful orange-brown capsules.

In this moss the capsule is nodding (cer'nuous) (Pl. III. fig. 15), and has a single peristome, consisting of sixteen equidistant teeth, each being deeply cut or cleft longitudinally (fig. 15 *a*), so that there are thirty-two teeth altogether; and these are marked with internal cross-bars, or transverse ridges. The calyptra is dimidiate (fig. 14); and the lid is furnished with a long oblique beak (fig. 15 *b*). The leaves are crowded, strongly nerved (fig. 12), lanceolate at the base, and very narrow towards the apex, which is toothed; they are, moreover, curved, and bent towards one side, or sécund.

Tor'tula murális (Pl. III. fig. 16) may be found on the top of almost every wall and on waste ground.

In this moss the peristome is single (fig. 18), consisting of thirty-two spirally twisted teeth, arranged in pairs. They are narrow and slender, and each is composed of two longitudinal portions (fig. 18 *a*), one of which is pale yellow, the other reddish brown, like the capsule, and both are fringed and covered with very minute papillæ. The capsule (fig. 18) is oblong, the ring or annulus remaining for some time. The lid is conical (fig. 19), with a longish somewhat oblique beak, and the calyptra is dimidiate (fig. 20). The stems are very short; the leaves (fig. 17) are oblong, obtuse; the nerve strong, and projecting as a colourless spirally striated bristle. The bristles often give the patches of the moss a hoary appearance on wall-tops. The margins of the leaves are folded back or recurved, giving them a peculiar thickened appearance.

The largest of our mosses are contained in the next genus, viz. *Polyt'richum*, some of them having the stems from 2 to 4 inches, or even more, in height; they are common on heaths and in woods.

Polyt'richum pilif'erum (Pl. III. fig. 22) is very common on open dry heaths. This moss has simple stems, with the leaves crowded on the lower part of those which are fertile or fruit-bearing. The fruit-stalk is terminal (acrocarpous); the capsule ovate, 4-sided or quadrangular, with a knob or struma (*strúma*, a swelling) at the base, the lid having a short beak. The calyptra (fig. 24) is half-cleft (dimidiate) and very hairy. The peristome is single, and consists of sixty-four teeth. The leaves (fig. 23) are lanceolate, nearly upright, the margins folded inwards or inflexed; and they end abruptly in a saw-edged or serrated hair-like point.

Poly'trichum commúne, which is also very common, is larger than the last species, and may easily be distinguished by the curved and serrate leaves, which have no bristle-point.

In the early spring, patches of both these mosses may be found, in which the stems are terminated by little rosettes (figs. 25 & 26); these will be referred to presently.

Keeping still to the end-fruited or Acrocarpous mosses, we have next to mention *Funa'ria hygro-met'rica* (Pl. III. figs. 28, 29), which is readily distinguished from most other mosses by the pale apple-green colour which it possesses before the capsule ripens. It is extremely common on walls and waste ground.

The capsule of this moss (fig. 31) differs from those of the preceding mosses in the peristome being double (fig. 42), or composed of an outer and an inner row of teeth. The outer row consists of sixteen oblique reddish teeth, which are marked with transverse bars or trabe'culæ (*trabecula*, a little beam), and their points are connected by a net-like thin plate. The inner row contains also sixteen teeth, arising from the division of the membrane lining the capsule; these are yellowish, thin, and placed opposite the outer teeth. The capsule itself is pear-shaped or pyriform, orange-red when ripe, curved, and with the mouth oblique. The calyptra (fig. 36) is half-cleft, and expanded as if blown out below. The lid (fig. 31 *a*) is convex and obtuse; and the annulus (fig. 39) is large and easily separable. The fruit-stalks are curved near the top. The leaves (fig. 30) are ovate, concave, entire, with a nerve reaching the apex, which is acute and prolonged into a little point, or apic'ulate. The spores (fig. 38) are small and reddish brown. The specific name (*hygromet'rica*) of this moss expresses its hygrometric property; for if either the recent and moist moss be dried or the dry moss wetted, the fruit-stalk gradually twists in opposite directions in the two cases.

The last of the Acrocarpous mosses which we shall notice, *Bry'um capil'lare* (Pl. III. fig. 49), is tolerably common on trunks of trees, on the ground, and sometimes on walls.

The capsule of this moss has a double peristome or mouth-fringe; the outer consisting of sixteen reddish-brown, equidistant, transversely striped teeth; the inner composed of sixteen thin keeled teeth, more or less split down the middle, and with two or three intermediate cilia. The capsule is nodding, smooth, oblong, pear-shaped, slightly narrowed below the mouth; the lid being somewhat convex, and furnished with a short slender beak. The calyptra is dimidiate. The leaves (fig. 50) are obovate, the nerve extending beyond the point, rendering them bristle-pointed. The seeds (fig. 49 *a*) are small and green.

This moss serves to illustrate a great difficulty, which will often occur to the student, in determining whether a moss is end-fruited or side-fruited. For in this, as in many other end-fruited mosses, a little side-shoot or young branch (innovation) grows from the main stem immediately below the leaves surrounding the base of the fruit-stalk, so that the fruit-stalk appears to arise from the side of the stem. The only method of overcoming the difficulty is to examine carefully the comparative size and thickness of the stem and the shoot, and to determine which is the weaker and so the newer. The leaves surrounding the base of the fruit-stalk, which are mostly somewhat different in structure from the stem-leaves, are called the *perichæ'tial* (περὶ, around, χαίτη, bristle) leaves.

From among the side-fruited or Pleurocarpous mosses we shall select one only, *Hyp'num rutab'ulum* (Pl. III. fig. 43), which is common on the trunks of trees and on banks.

In this moss, the nodding unequal curved capsule (fig. 45) has a double peristome, resembling that of *Bryum* (fig. 47). The calyptra is half-cleft, and the lid conical and shortly beaked. The stem is reclining or procumbent, and the pale green imbricated leaves (fig. 41) are ovate and pointed, faintly saw-edged, the nerve becoming indistinct at about the middle. It will be noticed that the cells of the leaf (fig. 48) have the prosenchymatous form, or are elongate with pointed ends; and that the fruit-stalk (fig. 45) is rough with little grains.

Fructification.—The fruit-producing organs of the mosses are of two kinds, comparable to those of the flowering plants, but with their names changed, as in the case of the ferns; the representatives of the anther being called antheridia, and those of the pistil archegonia. The antheridia may be best examined in *Polytrichum piliferum* or *commune,* the patches of stems with red rosette-like heads (figs. 25, 26) being readily found in the spring on open heaths. The coloured leaves forming these heads differ in form from those of the stem, being broader and very sharp-pointed, and have received the distinctive name of *perigónial* (περὶ, around, γόνος, offspring) leaves. In the centre of these leaves, which must be separated with mounted needles in a drop of water, the antheridia (fig. 27), forming oblong cellular green sacs, will be seen; and intermingled with them will be found some slender pale filaments, composed of mostly two rows of cells, which are the *paraph'yses* (παράφυσις, a side growth). If the antheridia are quite ripe, they swell somewhat in the water, and from the free or unattached end a very delicate, colourless, cellular mass gradually escapes. If the antheridia are not quite ripe, the mass must be liberated by dissection.

On carefully examining this mass under a high power, it will be seen to consist of very delicate rounded cells (fig. 3 *a*), each containing a coiled filament, revolving more or less rapidly. After a time, these filaments (fig. 3 *b*) escape, so that they may be examined more minutely. They are excessively delicate, and are best seen when dried on the slide. Each consists of a very slender curved filament, with a still finer filament, or cilium, arising from it on each side. These are the spermatozóa or spermatozóids (σπέρμα, seed, ζῶον, animal, εἶδος, resemblance).

In *Funária* the antheridia (fig. 37) may also be found, by careful examination, in the little green heads terminating some of the stems (fig. 41, of the natural size). In this moss, the paraphyses are inflated at the summit into little knobs, or they are capitate (fig. 37). The pistil-like organs of mosses, or the *archegónia,* from which the capsule is formed, must be looked for in the winter or early spring.

They occur in the parts of the stems from which the fruit-stalk subsequently arises, and are surrounded by perichætial leaves, so as to resemble in general aspect the antheridial heads. They are readily found in *Tortula* and *Funaria*, which are always at hand.

The archegonia (Pl. III. fig. 21) differ in form from the antheridia, being flask-shaped, with a neck and a dilated base. The neck contains a slender canal, and within the base is a special embryonal cell, from which the capsule is subsequently formed. The spermatozoa of the antheridia pass down the canals of the archegonia, and fertilize the embryonal cells ; but one archegonium only comes to maturity in each head, the others ceasing to grow, and withering, in which condition they are found at the base of the fruit-stalk when the capsule is fully formed. The embryonal cell grows by subdivision, so as to form a stalk-like body, which as it rises extends the archegonium upwards until it splits across near the base. Thus the archegonium becomes split horizontally into two parts, the upper and longer of which forms the calyptra, whilst the lower remains as a very short tube or sheath (*vagi'nula*) surrounding the base of the fruit-stalk. The cellular stalk-like body then swells at the summit, the swollen portion gradually becoming developed into the capsule, by resolving itself into an outer wall lined inside with a coat forming the outer row of teeth at the top, and within this a thinner membrane or spore-sac, the cleft upper margin of which forms the inner teeth; and within this are contained the spores. The mass of cells within the spore-sac remains, forming a central column, called the *columella*.

These stages of growth may be readily traced in *Funaria*. In Plate III., fig. 40 represents two fertilized archegonia of the natural size, surrounded by the perichætial leaves; fig. 33 is a still more advanced archegone. In fig. 34 the calyptra has separated from the vaginule, and contains the stalk-like body, which is represented alone in fig. 32, the dark summit indicating the commencing formation of the capsule. Fig. 35 represents the young capsule, in which all the parts are more advanced in growth.

When the seeds of mosses germinate, they produce at first a green *Conferva*-like filament, which branches at one end, the cells containing green endochrome, while brownish little roots are given off from the other end. The young leafy buds or young stems arise from these confervoid filaments.

Examination.—In the examination of the mosses, the capsules should be viewed as opake objects while fixed in the forceps; and to discover the minute structure of the teeth of the peristome, a capsule should be wetted with spirit, then immersed in water, slit up with fine scissors, and spread out with the mounted needles, so as to form a transparent object. In this way, the curious structure of the teeth becomes very distinct.

It must be noticed that, in the mosses, the antheridia and the archegonia usually occur in separate flower-like heads; or the mosses are either monœcious or diœcious (p. 38).

Preservation.—The mosses may be dried under pressure, and preserved entire in the same manner as the ferns or the flowering plants. If simply dried without pressure, their structure can be readily made out at any future time, by immersing them in water, or by keeping them for a few hours in a moist atmosphere. The minute structures of mosses may be mounted in solution of chloride of calcium, or in glycerine; they keep extremely well without closing the cells.

CHAPTER VII.

ALGÆ (ALGA, SEA-WEED).

THE plants belonging to the Class Algæ grow in water, either in that of the sea or in fresh water; a few of them, however, being found on damp earth, damp walls, &c. The marine Algæ are commonly known as sea-weeds; but the fresh-water Algæ generally receive but little popular notice, forming, as they do, slimy masses or strata, of a green or brownish, sometimes red, colour.

Algæ are of simple structure, consisting entirely of cells; in some these are single, in others, united end to end, to form threads or filaments, or grouped into a leaf-like expansion, or collected few together into a little spherical group or a flat plate. They possess none of the fibres, vessels, or ducts of the higher plants, although some long and slender cells, existing in the stalks of the fronds of the larger kinds, bear considerable resemblance to woody fibre. They exhibit no distinction of stem and leaf, but consist of fronds representing the stem and leaf combined and undistinguishable. And the term frond must be understood to signify the separate parts arising from the point of attachment when they are fixed; and in the case of those which are unattached or free, the entire plant is called a frond.

The Algæ are divided into three Orders, viz. the Fucoid'eæ or olive-coloured Algæ, the Florid'eæ or red, and the Confervoid'eæ or green Algæ.

FUCOID'EÆ, Fucoid Algæ, or Melanospor'eæ (μέλας, black or dark). The plants composing this order form our largest sea-weeds, and are found everywhere

PLATE IV. [PAGE 64.]

MARINE ALGÆ.

Fig.
1. *Dasya coccinea,* piece of.
2. *Dasya coccinea,* portion with capsule (ceramidium).
3. *Dasya coccinea,* portion of main filament.
4. *Dasya coccinea,* section of filament.
5. *Melobesia polymorpha.*
6. *Melobesia polymorpha,* portion with capsules (ceramidia).
7. *Jania rubens.*
8. *Jania rubens.*
9. *Lithocystis Allmanni.*
10. *Ceramium nodosum.*
11. *Ceramium nodosum,* filament.
12. *Ceramium rubrum,* filament.
13. *Ceramium rubrum,* tetraspore.
14. *Ceramium rubrum,* end of filament.
15. *Ceramium rubrum,* capsule (favella).
16. *Fucus vesiculosus,* receptacles of.
17. *Fucus vesiculosus,* capsules (conceptacles).
18. *Fucus serratus,* antheridial conceptacles.
19. Spore of *Fucus vesiculosus.*

Fig.
20. Antheridia of *Fucus serratus.*
21. *Plocamium coccineum,* sporophyll.
22. *Plocamium coccineum,* with capsule (coccidium).
23. *Plocamium coccineum,* portion of frond.
24. *Plocamium coccineum,* tetraspore from sporophyll.
25. *Polysiphonia fastigiata,* portion of.
26. *Polysiphonia fastigiata,* filament with capsules (ceramidia).
27. *Polysiphonia fastigiata,* portion of filament.
28. *Corallina officinalis.*
29. *Corallina officinalis,* portion of filament.
30. *Corallina officinalis,* capsule (ceramidium).
31. *Enteromorpha compressa.*
32. *Enteromorpha compressa,* cells of frond.
33. *Hypnea purpurascens,* capsule (coccidium).
34. *Hypnea purpurascens,* spores.
35. *Hypnea purpurascens,* filament.

Plate IV.

in the sea and on the sea-shore. They are of an olive-green or olive-brown colour, and usually become darker on drying.

Fúcus vesiculósus, with its parallel-sided or linear olive-brown fronds, is known to every one as the sea-weed which is hung up to act as a weather-glass. The fronds have a central stout vein, or midrib, and scattered air-bladders, mostly in pairs.

The fructification consists of yellowish oval enlargements of the ends of the fronds, called the *receptacles* (fig. 16); but these are somewhat variable in form, being often angular or truncate. On holding one of the receptacles to the light, it will appear to contain a number of little grains imbedded in its substance, slightly projecting above the surface, and in the centre of each is a minute dot or pore. These grains are the capsules, or *conceptacles,* and contain the spores. The substance of the receptacles is composed of a beautiful network of colourless, jointed, cellular fibres (figs. 17 *a* and 18 *a*), the meshes of which are filled with a transparent gelatinous substance; but immediately around the conceptacles the cells are shorter and more closely packed. The spores (fig. 19) are arranged in the conceptacles in a radiate manner; they are brown, and surrounded by a colourless sac, called the *perispore* (περὶ, around, σπορά, seed); and between them are numerous slender, colourless, jointed, filaments, the *paraph'yses.* The spores are not, however, truly single spores, for they ultimately divide into eight segments or sporules, each of which is capable of producing a new plant.

In the conceptacles of some fronds of *Fucus* no spores will be found, the conceptacles (fig. 18) being filled with elegantly branched colourless filaments (fig. 20), the ends of many of them being distended into little yellowish sacs; these are the *antherid'ia.* The antheridia contain large numbers of exceedingly minute spermatozoa, furnished with two cilia, and

very similar to those existing in the antheridia of the
mosses; these, escaping through the pore of the conceptacle, fertilize the spores.

The figure (20) in the plate was drawn from a conceptacle of *Fucus serrátus*, another common species,
differing from *F. vesiculosus* in having the margins of
the frond serrate; the antheridia of the two species
do not, however, differ in any important respect.
To examine the conceptacles of *Fucus* and their contents, the receptacles should be soaked in water, if
not fresh, and thin sections made with a sharp knife.
They form very beautiful objects, and may be preserved in chloride of calcium or glycerine.

FLORID'EÆ, or Rhodosper'meæ (ῥόδον, rose, σπέρμα, seed).—The second Order of Algæ, forming the
Florideæ (*flos*, a flower), comprises the red sea-weeds;
a few of them are purple, or greenish-red; so that by
the colour alone they may be readily distinguished
from the Fucoids, and from nearly all those of the
next Order, the Confer'voids. A few of them are leaf-
like, or possess flat fronds; but most of them consist
of finely divided or feathery fronds. They are often
found upon the sea-shore of a dirty white colour, the
colouring matter having been decomposed or washed
out by rain.

We shall consider a few of the genera and species
under the heads of the families to which they belong.

CORALLINA'CEÆ, the Corallines, or calcareous Algæ.
—In this family we have the beautiful *Corallína offi-
cinális* (Pl. IV. fig. 28), the common Coralline, which
is very abundant on the sea-shore, attached to larger
sea-weeds, shells, and rocks. It is hard and chalky,
from the presence of a large proportion of carbonate
of lime in its minute cells. The fronds are composed
of jointed and branched filaments. The fructification
(figs. 29 and 30) consists of ovate cellular capsules, or
ceramid'ia (κεράμιον, earthen vessel), placed mostly
at the ends of pinnate stalks, and containing a tuft

of somewhat club-shaped jointed spores, springing
from the base of the capsules (fig. 30). When ripe,
the spores escape from a pore or hole in the end of
the capsules. The spores are 4-jointed, and hence
are called *tet'raspores* (τέτρα, *four*).

To observe these spores, the capsules must be soaked
in strong vinegar for some hours, and then washed
with water, to dissolve the calcareous matter.

Jánia rúbens (Pl. IV. figs. 7 and 8) is another
common and very elegant little coralline, and is of a
pale red colour. It differs from the last in the branches
being dichot'omous (δίχα, in two, τομὸς, cutting) or
forked, instead of pinnate. The capsules, or ceramidia,
have also two short horn-like branchlets, placed one
on each side, near the end.

The genus *Melobésia* has the frond crustaceous, *i. e.*
forming a hard crust or layer. *M. polymor'pha* (Pl.
IV. figs. 5 and 6) is common on shells, stones, &c.
The capsules (ceramidia) here form little blunt cones,
scattered over the crusts, and containing the tufted
tetraspores, as in *Corallina*.

Lithocys'tis Allman'ni (fig. 9) is very minute, and
not uncommon upon sea-weeds, stones, &c. It consists of a single fan-shaped crustaceous layer of cells,
closely investing the body to which it is attached; its
fructification is unknown.

Leaving the family of crustaceous Florideæ, we
shall now pass to those of softer consistence, although
all the marine Algæ contain a considerable quantity
of calcareous matter.

RHODOMELA'CEÆ.—In this family we have the large
genus *Polysiphónia*, in which the frond (Pl. IV. figs. 25
and 26) is filamentous, the filaments being apparently
jointed and longitudinally striated. The filaments
are composed of rings of cells (fig. 27), arranged end
to end, and containing dark endochrome. The ends
of the colourless cell-walls separating the endochromes
of the cells of adjacent rings produce the jointed ap-

pearance; while the striated appearance is caused by the dark cells being elongate and the cell-walls thick, so as to form white interspaces.

The fructification consists of capsules (ceramidia), attached to the sides of the branches, containing pear-shaped spores, with tetraspores imbedded in swollen branches of separate plants.

Polysiphónia fastigiáta (fig. 25, a small piece) is common, attached to the fronds of *Fucus*. Its filaments are rigid, bristle-like, of the same breadth throughout, forked, and forming globular brown or yellowish tufts, from 2 to 4 inches long. The joints are broader than long, each with 16–18 of the dark cells. In the centre of the branches of this sea-weed is a row of curious objects (fig. 26 *a*), consisting of a dark-coloured body surrounded with irregular spiny marginal processes, and with a colourless short process above and below. These require further investigation.

P. nigres'cens is also common among masses of sea-weeds. Its filaments are brown, pinnate, the branches awl-shaped, and the joints about as long as broad.

Dásya coccin'ea (Pl. IV. figs. 1 and 2, representing small portions of a filament) is a very common filamentous red sea-weed of the same family. The filaments are 6–8 inches long, and bipinnate,—the larger ones somewhat resembling those of *Polysiphonia*, in being composed of parallel longitudinal cells, arranged round the centre, but containing also smaller intermediate cells; while the smallest branches (fig. 2), which arise in tufts, consist of a single row of cells, little longer than broad. The fruit consists of ovate capsules (ceramidia), placed at the base of the branches, and containing a round mass of spores. There is also another kind of fructification, occurring on distinct plants; this is formed of one or two rows of tetraspores, immersed in pod-like capsules, called *stichid'ia* (στίχος, row).

DELESSERIA'CEÆ.—In this family, the typical or most highly developed genus of which, *Delesséria*, has beautiful leaf-like rose-red fronds, we shall examine the common *Plocámium coccin'eum* (Pl. IV. figs. 23 and 22). This is of a fine red colour; the fronds are from 2 to 12 inches long, and consist of numerous branched and bushy filaments. These are compressed, with the branchlets arranged in alternate rows on the two margins of the stem. The end branchlets are acute and pectinate (*pecten*, a comb), or arranged like the teeth of a comb. The cells of which the filaments consist are small and angular, giving the surface the appearance of being elegantly netted under a high power. The fruit (fig. 22) consists of globular capsules, called *coccid'ia* (κόκκος, a berry), placed in the axils or forks at which two branches separate, and containing a mass of angular spores. There are also tetraspore-pods (stichidia), as in *Dasya*; and tetra-spores (fig. 24) in little leaf-like altered branches (fig. 21), called *spor'ophylles* (σπορὰ, seed, φύλλον, leaf), and antheridia are present.

RHODYMENIA'CEÆ.—In this family we have *Hyp'nea purpuras'cens* (Pl. IV. fig. 35). The filamentous pale purple frond of this sea-weed is from 6 inches to a foot or more in length, the branches being alternate and spreading. The fructification consists of capsules or coccidia (fig. 32), immersed in the branches, and containing the spores (fig. 34). Tetraspores also occur in the cells of the surface of the filaments.

CERAMIA'CEÆ.—This is the last family to be noticed. *Cerámium nodósum* (Pl. IV. figs. 10 and 11), which belongs to it, is a most delicate and elegant filament-ous sea-weed, commonly found attached to other sea-weeds. The filaments are hair-like or capillary, irre-gularly dichot'omous; they consist of colourless cells, 3 or 4 times as long as broad, and with thick walls. The junctions of the cells are swollen (fig. 11), and covered with very minute dark red cells, giving them a knotty and jointed appearance to the naked eye or under a low power. The globular capsules, or *favel'læ* (*favus*, a honeycomb), containing the numerous spores, are situated at the ends of the branchlets, and the tetraspores (fig. 11) in twos or threes on the outer margins of them.

In *Cerámium rúbrum*, which is also very common, being found attached to stones, rocks, and the larger Algæ, the filaments (Pl. IV. fig. 12) are stouter than in *C. nodosum*, branched so as to form tufts from 2 to 10 inches long, and their ends forked, with the tips hooked inwards (fig. 14). The central cells of the filaments are large and rounded, and their walls are entirely covered with a layer of very small angular red cells. The globular capsules (fig. 15), or *favellæ*, are situated on the suter surface of the branches, stalked, and supported by 3 or 4 short branchlets. The tetraspores (fig. 13) are imbedded in the branches, towards the ends. The capsules called favellæ differ from the coccidia in the walls being simply membranous, while the walls of the coccidia, like those of the ceramidia, are composed of cells.

The tetraspores are usually imbedded. among the cells of the superficial layer of the filaments, and are not very easily recognized by an unpractised eye; it will be observed in the figures that they are sometimes cleft horizontally, at others obliquely.

CONFERVOID'EÆ.—This Order consists principally of the green freshwater Algæ, although some of them are yellowish brown, purple, or red, and some are marine. Their general structure may be best illustrated by selecting certain common examples from the families composing the order. The families are 13 in number. The species which are figured in the plates are found in fresh water, except when otherwise stated.

CONFERVA'CEÆ.—On removing some of the soft green matter found adhering to the stems of water-

PLATE V. [PAGE 70.]

FRESHWATER ALGÆ.

Fig.
1. *Conferva floccosa,* single filament.
2. *Lyngbya muralis,* single filament.
3. *Ulothrix mucosa* (?), filament.
4. *Synedra radians,* prepared frustules.
5. *Synedra radians,* tuft of natural frustules.
6. *Cladophora crispata,* with zoospores (*a*).
7. *Batrachospermum moniliforme,* portion of filament.
8. *Batrachospermum moniliforme,* filament.
9. *Closterium acerosum.*
10. *Draparnaldia glomerata.*
11. *Spirogyra quinina.*
12. *Spirogyra nitida,* filaments conjugating.
13. *Zygnema cruciata.*
14. *Coleochæte scutata.*
15. *Xanthidia* in flint.
16. *Micrasterias rotata.*
17. *Gomphonema acuminatum.*

Fig.
18. *Gomphonema acuminatum,* prepared frustules.
19. *Ankistrodesmus falcatus.*
20. *Pediastrum Boryanum.*
21. *Hyalotheca dissiliens.*
22. *Pinnularia viridis.*
23. *Fragilaria capucina.*
24. *Fragilaria capucina,* prepared frustules; s^* side view of *F. virescens.*
25. *Scenedesmus quadricauda.*
26. *Schizogonium,* probably a form of *Lyngbya.*
27. *Campylodiscus costatus.*
28. *Nitzschia minutissima,* front view.
29. *Nitzschia minutissima,* valves.
30. *Epithemia turgida.*
31. *Diatoma elongatum,* natural frustules.
32. *Diatoma elongatum,* prepared frustules.
33. *Cocconeis placentula.*

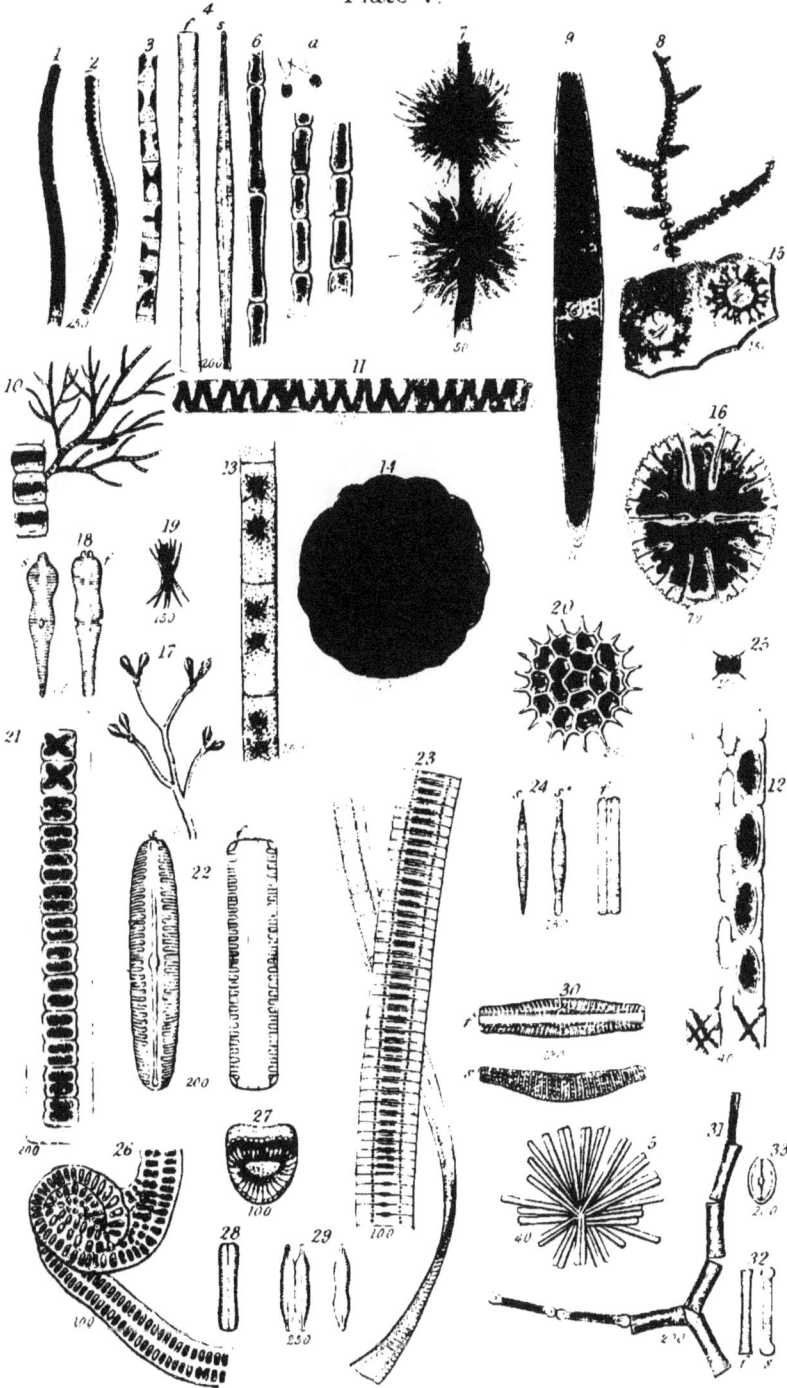

Plate V.

plants in any pool or pond, one of the species of *Conferva*, *C. flocculosa*, is almost sure to be met with. On close inspection with the naked eye, the green filaments of which it consists are just visible, as extremely fine, soft, silky threads ; and, under a high power of the microscope, the filaments are seen to be unbranched, and composed of a single row of cells (Pl. V. fig. 1), or joints, as they are called in technical works ; these are 2 or 3 times as long as broad. In some specimens the joints are swollen, so as to present a rounded outline. In another common species, *C. bombyc'ina*, the filaments are somewhat more slender, and the joints are from 3 to 5 times as long as broad.

Cladoph'ora crispáta.—This Confervoid forms large, entangled, dull-green masses, composed of branched, tufted, somewhat rigid and coarse filaments. It is often a troublesome overrunner of the fresh-water vivarium. The filaments are composed of thick-walled cells (Pl. V. fig. 6), from 4 to 6 times as long as broad, and often containing minute starch-granules.

The Confervaceæ have two modes of reproduction. The first of these consists in the division of the endochrome of the joints into a number of distinct segments, each of which becomes furnished at one end with two very slender cilia (Pl. V. fig. 6 *a*). After a time, these ciliated bodies, which are called *zo'ospores* (ζῶον, animal, σπορὰ, seed) or *gonid'ia* (γονὴ, seed, εἶδος, resemblance), escape from the cells either by their rupture or through a papillary orifice, and swim about in the water, ultimately losing their cilia and growing into cells resembling those of the parent plant. In the second method, which occurs, for instance, in *Conferva bombycina*, certain of the joints enlarge so as to become rounded or inflated ; their endochrome then becomes coated with a new cell-wall, and so forms a spore, which subsequently escapes from the cell and germinates.

CHÆTOPHORA'CEÆ.—*Draparnal' dia glomeráta* forms

small green jelly-like masses, adhering to sticks and
stones in water. These consist of branched filaments
(Pl. V. fig. 10), prolonged at the ends into colourless
hair-like points, and composed of single rows of cells,
the green endochrome forming a band across the
middle of each cell, the ends being colourless.

In *Coleochæ'te scutáta* (Pl. V. fig. 14) the cells are
closely united, so as to form a minute flat green disk.
In the natural state, this beautiful little object adheres
to the submerged leaves and stems of water-plants,
and is therefore difficult to be found. But if a few
healthy water-plants be kept for some time in a glass
jar, the little *Coleochæte*, which is about as large as
a pin's head, will often be found adhering to the side
of the glass.

BAT'RACHOSPER'MEÆ.—The members of this family
resemble to the naked eye the little masses of *Draparnaldia*, and they are found in the same localities.
They are of various colours, being green, brown,
purple, or red. They consist, as in *Bat'rachosper'mum
monilifor'me* (Pl. V. fig. 8), of branched filaments,
which have a knotty appearance under a low power.
The larger filaments are composed of cells arranged
end to end, the knots consisting of numerous smaller
whorled filaments, *i. e.* filaments arising from around
them at the same level (fig. 7). The cells composing
the whorled filaments are beaded or moniliform, and
are prolonged into colourless hair-like points. The
globules seen among the branches (fig. 7) consist of
groups of spores.

ZYGNEMA'CEÆ.—The members of this family resemble the Confervaceæ in consisting of simple cellular filaments (Pl. V. figs. 11, 13), but differ from them
in the elegant arrangement of the endochrome: this
forms beautiful spiral bands, as in *Spirog'yra quini'na*
(fig. 11), or star-shaped masses, as in *Zygne'ma cru-
cia'ta* (fig. 13). A remarkably curious phenomenon
met with in them is the manner in which the spores are

formed, and which is known as *conjugation*. In this process the opposite cells of two distinct filaments, lying near together, push out protrusions of the cell-walls, which meet and open into each other, forming cross tubes, as in *Spirog'yra nit'ida* (Pl. V. fig. 12). The contents of the opposite cells of the filaments then unite, forming large spores, which remain either in the cells of one of the filaments or in the cross tubes.

The three species figured are common in clear pools.

DESMIDIA'CEÆ.—The Desmidiaceæ are truly microscopic, few of them being even perceptible to the naked eye without the very closest examination. They are very beautiful, on account of their bright green colour and often elegant forms. Many of them are very common, existing in every pond or ditch; but they abound most in clear open boggy pools on heaths. On placing some water containing them in a glass jar and exposing it to the light, they will often be found adhering to the glass, or forming a layer on the surface of the muddy sediment.

The Desmidiaceæ consist mostly of single cells (Pl. V. figs. 9, 16); and these consist of two equal halves or segments, as indicated either by a paleness of the endochrome or a deep constriction at the line of junction, which is called the *suture*. The cells are often elegantly lobed and cut, or spiny; and in many the surface exhibits minute markings, consisting of little protrusions of the cell-wall outwards, or inflations, as they are called.

Their reproduction is effected by division and conjugation. In the process of division the cells gradually separate at the suture, and a new half-cell is formed upon each old half, which grows until it attains the size and form of the original half of the parent-cell. The conjugation is effected by two cells approximating so that their sutures are near together, the cells then

H

open at the sutures, and the effused contents become
united to form a spore or sporange, from which one
or more individuals are formed. These spores are
often elegantly spinous on the surface.

Among the species selected for illustration is *Clos-
térium acerósum* (Pl. V. fig. 9), in which the cells are
single, elongate, very slightly curved or lunate; the
endochrome forms long bands, often containing numerous globules or transparent vesicles. At each
end of the cells is a round transparent vesicle, containing exceedingly minute granules, which exhibit a
trembling kind of motion. Between the cell-wall
and the cell-contents very fine currents may also be
detected, forming a circulation resembling that in the
hairs of *Tradescantia*.

In *Micrastérias rotáta* (Pl. V. fig. 16) the cells,
which are single, are deeply cleft into two segments
at the suture, the segments being again regularly cut
into five lobes, which are toothed or dentate.

In *Hyalothéca dissil'iens* (Pl. V. fig. 21) the cells
are united into a cylindrical filament, and are surrounded by a very delicate gelatinous sheath. In
Ankistrodes'mus falcátus (Pl. V. fig. 19) the cells resemble those of *Closterium* in shape, but are aggregated into faggot-like bundles, and are very much
smaller. In the beautiful little *Pedias'trum boryánum*
(Pl. V. fig. 20) the cells are aggregated into a disk,
the marginal cells being bidentate or having each two
points, so that the whole resembles a star. The species
of *Pediastrum* are reproduced by the contents of each
cell subdividing into numerous ciliated segments or
zoospores, which subsequently escape in a mass from
the cell, ultimately losing their cilia, and reuniting
to form a new individual.

In *Scenedes'mus quadricau'da* (Pl. V. fig. 25) the
oblong cells are united, side by side, the outermost
cells being furnished with a bristle at each end. The
division of these cells takes place obliquely, so that

in the divided groups the cells are situated in two alternate rows.

The spores of many of the Desmidiaceæ are spinous, and they are often found fossil in flint (Pl. V. fig. 15). To detect them in this substance, thin slips of flint may be examined under a half-inch power; or the chips of flint may be cemented to a slide with balsam, and ground down on a hone.

The Desmidiaceæ must be mounted in the moist state : the smaller ones will keep well in chloride of calcium; but the larger ones are injured both by that liquid and by glycerine. The remarks made upon mounting, at page 15, are especially applicable to these delicate organisms.

DIATOMA'CEÆ, or Siliceous Algæ.—The members of this family are singly very minute; but when existing in large numbers, as they are often found at the bottom of ditches and ponds, on the submerged stems of water-plants, or upon damp ground, they form yellowish-brown evident masses or strata. They occur both in sea- and in fresh water. They usually consist, like the Desmidiaceæ, of single cells, which are called frustules. But they are especially characterized by the cell-walls being imbued with silica or flint, so that if the frustules be heated to redness upon the point of a knife or a slip of platinum-foil, which destroys the organic part of the cells, the coat of silica remains, exhibiting the perfect form of the original cells or frustules. The form of the frustules is very different in the various genera and species, as represented in Pl. V. figs. 22, 23, 27, 30, 31, and Pl. VI. figs. 16, 17, 23; and it will be noticed that, in the figures, two views are given of each frustule, *f* indicating the front view, and *s* the side view. In all the front views, as in Pl. V. fig. 22, one or more lines will be observed running longitudinally down the middle of the frustules, and corresponding to the indications of division existing in the cells of the

Desmidiaceæ. Each half of a frustule is called a *valve,* and the line at which these valves meet is called the *suture.* That side or aspect of the frustule in which the suture lies (fig. 22*f*) is the *front view;* and the other aspect of the frustule (fig. 22 *s*) is the *side view.* The frustules are mostly four-sided—the main breadths of the two opposite valves forming two sides, and the bent margins of the valves, with the back and front of the hoop, forming the two other sides; so that the view presented by the side of a frustule is the same as that of a single valve. The suture is the line at which the division of the frustules takes place in the formation of new individuals. In this process the cell-contents divide into two parts, as in ordinary endogenous cell-formation,—the two new surfaces thus produced becoming coated with a new portion of cell-wall or valve, so that two frustules now occupy the place of the original one. At the same time a siliceous band, encircling the frustules at the line of suture, is formed to fill up the interval between the edges of the parent valves; this is the *hoop* (Pl. V. fig. 22*f;* Pl. VI. fig. 10*f*), and beneath it lie the two newly formed valves. In many cases I believe that each half-frustule becomes coated with a new entire cell-wall, with its siliceous valves.

The frustules of the Diatomaceæ are constantly undergoing division when in vigorous growth. After the frustules have divided, the new ones either separate entirely, as is perhaps most commonly the case; or they remain united, sometimes completely, so as to constitute a filament (Pl. V. fig. 23), while at others the frustules cohere only at the angles (Pl. VI. fig. 23), so as to form a zigzag chain.

In some species, the frustules are attached to foreign bodies by means of a gelatinous cushion (Pl. V. fig. 5 ; Pl. VI. fig. 7) ; while in others they are situated upon a simple or branched gelatinous stalk (Pl. V. fig. 17) or stipes (*stipes,* a stem).

When the frustules are examined in the living state, the cell-contents resemble those of ordinary vegetable cells, excepting in regard to the colour, and exhibit granules and globules, and sometimes a nucleus is visible. It will also be noticed that many of the free frustules move slowly across the field of the microscope; but the cause of the motion is unknown.

When the frustules have been properly prepared, the surface of the valves exhibits a number of coarser or finer markings, consisting of dots, lines (striæ), flutings, or networks, &c., arranged with great regularity and symmetry, often of extreme minuteness, and rendering them exquisite objects under the microscope. The exhibition of these markings requires not only that the valves shall be properly prepared and mounted, but that the object-glasses be of good quality, and that the management of the light be thoroughly understood; so that to a beginner, their examination is often a matter of great difficulty; for only the very coarsest or largest of these markings can be perceived in the natural frustules.

The appearance of these markings, and even their apparent absence or presence, frequently depends upon the kind of illumination used: thus, under one kind of illumination the valves may appear simply white or coloured, while under another they appear covered with lines, and under a third with dots. It will often be observed, also, that the colour of the valves varies according to the illumination and the power used—the same valve appearing white, yellow, brown, blue, &c; and the wet or dry state of the frustules often cause a decided difference in their appearance as regards colour.

To illustrate the forms and markings of the frustules and valves, we may select the following species taking first those which occur in fresh water.

In *Epithémia tur'gida* (Pl. V. fig. 30), the side-view or valve (*s*) exhibits transverse or slightly radia-

ting lines, with intermediate rows of dots—these
markings being continued over the margins of the
valves so as to appear also in the front view (fig. 30 f),
ceasing at the hoop. The frustules are curved or
arcuate (*ar'cus*, a bow) in the side view, oblong and
narrowed at the ends in the front view.

In *Fragilária capucína* (Pl. V. fig. 23), which is extremely common in fresh-water pools, &c., the frustules are united side by side into long filaments,
which are often twisted. In the separate and prepared frustule, the front view (Pl. V. fig. 24 f) is rectangular, the valves (*s*) being narrowly lance-shaped
or lanceolate. The valves under ordinary illumination appear colourless and without markings, but, by
proper management of the light, very fine transverse
striæ are seen upon them, consisting of rows of very
minute dots. Fig. 24 s* represents the valve of *Fragilaria vires'cens*, a nearly allied species.

Diat'oma elongátum (Pl. V. fig. 31) is often found
with the above. Its frustules are coherent at the
angles. The front view (fig. 32 f) is rectangular,
often slightly narrowed in the middle; and the valves
are narrowly linear, and capitate at the ends; they
are also transversely striated.

In *Synédra splen'dens* (Pl. V. fig. 5) the frustules
radiate from a soft gelatinous cushion. They are
linear in the front view (fig. 4 f), the valves (fig. 4 s)
being gradually narrowed or attenuated from the
middle to the ends, and exhibit transverse striæ
interrupted opposite a middle longitudinal line.

In *Campylodis'cus costátus* (Pl. V. fig. 27) the frustules are disk-shaped and curved, so as somewhat to
resemble a saddle. The markings consist of central
dots, with radiating coarse flutings.

Nitzsch'ia minutis'sima (Pl. V. fig. 28) has oblique
valves, *i. e.* the front half of the suture is not opposite
the back portion; the valves (fig. 29) are constricted
in the middle, and the ends narrowed and prolonged.

The markings consist of a row of oblong dots or puncta (*punctum*, a point). This species often forms yellowish layers upon damp paths, &c.

In the next group, the valves have a longitudinal line running down the middle of the valves, with a little knob or nodule in its centre (Pl. V. fig. 22 *s*), both consisting of internal thickened portions of the valves.

In *Cocconéis placen'tula* (Pl. V. fig. 33) the valves are oval, and the markings consist of longitudinal rows of minute dots, with a marginal row of puncta; these markings are invisible under ordinary illumination.

In *Gomphonéma acuminátum* (Pl. V. fig. 17) the frustules are attached to a branched stalk (stipes); they are wedge-shaped or cúneate (*cúneus*, a wedge) and transversely striate (fig. 18), the striæ consisting of dots.

In *Pinnulária vir'idis* (Pl. V. fig. 22), which is very often seen slowly traversing the field of the microscope when a drop of pond-water is examined, the frustules in the front view are linear, the valves being elliptic oblong, and transversely striated, the striæ consisting of furrows.

In *Gyrosig'ma* (*Pleurosig'ma*) *attenuátum* (Pl. VI. fig. 16) the valves are sigmoid, or somewhat resemble a Greek ς (sigma) in outline, and the markings consist of rectangularly crossed rows of very fine dots; in the front view, the frustules are linear-oblong with truncate ends.

. *Tabellária flocculósa* (Pl. VI. fig. 23) has the frustules adherent only at the angles, as in *Diátoma*. They are rectangular, and in the front view exhibit a row of longitudinal dark lines interrupted in the middle; these have been compared to the vittæ of the fruit of the Umbelliferæ, and have received the same name.

Among the marine species may be mentioned *Melosíra nummuloídes* (Pl. VI. fig. 9), in which the frustules are united into a chain or cylindrical filament. This is very common among sea-weeds, &c.;

and it illustrates well the process of division of the frustules (fig. 10 f). The valves are covered with fine dots, and near each end of the frustules is a projecting rim encircling it, and appearing as a curved line extending beyond the margin of the frustule in the front view. In *Actinocy'clus undulátus* (Pl. VI. fig. 5) the frustules are separate, disk-shaped, and the valves are divided into six equal parts by six rays, each alternate portion of the surface of the valves being situated on a lower level than those adjacent, so that an alteration in the focus is required to bring into view the dots on any two adjacent divisions of the valve. The surface of the valves is covered with easily recognized dots. The form of the surface is best seen in the front view (fig. 5 f) when the frustule is placed on its edge.

Rhabdonéma arcuátum (Pl. VI. fig. 7), which is very commonly found attached to sea-weeds, resembles *Tabellária* in the frustules having the vittæ (Pl. VI. fig. 8f). The frustules form short filaments, attached by a little gelatinous cushion. The valves have transverse striæ, interrupted in the middle (fig. 8 s).

Gyrosig'ma (Pleurosig'ma) angulátum (Pl. VI. fig. 17) resembles *G. attenuátum* in the sigmoid form; but the markings consist of lines crossing each other obliquely; and these are resolvable into rows of dots (fig. 17 a) under suitable illumination.

In *Coscinodis'cus radiátus* (Pl. VI. fig. 3) the frustules are disk-shaped, the valves being elegantly sculptured with easily recognized cell-like markings or dots, so as to resemble a piece of vegetable cellular tissue. But in some other species the dots are very minute, and difficult to be shown satisfactorily. These markings consist of depressions or pits in the surface of the valves. That this is the case may easily be seen by examining a fragment of the valve, when the shadings of the broken ends of the netted thicker portions, which project like teeth, strongly contrast with the difficultly distinguishable portions of the thin interspaces. The fossil forms from the Bermuda deposit are best for the investigation of this structure; many of these are extremely beautiful microscopic objects, their markings resembling those on the engine-turned back of a watch.

The detection of the finer markings of the Diatomaceæ, which, according to my view, consist of depressions like those upon the valves of *Coscinodiscus*, is a matter of great difficulty to those who are unaccustomed to the use of the microscope, and who have not a complete set of apparatus. The main point to be attended to in bringing them into view, is to use one-sided oblique light, *i. e.* to turn the mirror by its stem as much as possible to one side, and then to incline it so as to throw the light upon the object. In this way the valves of the species of *Gyrosigma*, for instance, appear covered with lines (Pl. VI. figs. 16 and 17); but the lines are spurious, *i. e.* they are the optical expression of rows of minute dots (figs. 16 *a*, 17 *a*); and when oblique light is thrown upon the valves from all sides, by means of a special achromatic condenser, in which the central rays are excluded, the dots become distinct, and the markings resemble those on the valves of *Coscinodiscus*. To show the finer dots clearly, a valve should be crushed, so as to obtain a fragment as flat as possible; for the surface of the valves is curved more or less in all the species. The valves of *G. angulatum* are generally used to test the quality of the object-glasses of the microscope, and also for practice in "making out" the lines and dots; there are, however, many Diatomaceæ more difficult.

As the nature of these markings is a disputed point, the discussion of which is not adapted for an elementary work, I must refer for further details to the 'Micrographic Dictionary;' it may be remarked, however, that some observers have regarded them as cells, and others as elevations or tubercles on the surface of the valves.

The preparation of the valves for showing the markings should be effected by burning the frustules, or the mass containing them, on a strip of platinum-foil over a spirit-lamp. The incinerated mass should then be transferred to a slide, and the valves separated with the greatest care by a bristle mounted in a hair-pencil stick under a low power of the microscope.

This is, however, a substitute for the proper method, which is dangerous in the hands of one unpractised in chemical manipulation. It is this:—The mass of Diatomaceæ (the water containing it having been carefully poured off as far as possible) is put into a Florence oil-flask, and strong nitric acid (aquafortis) gently added, more than sufficient to cover it. The mixture is then carefully boiled over a spirit-lamp for some time. When it is cold, distilled water is added, the whole shaken, and allowed to settle. The watery part is then gently poured off, more water added, and this poured off after settling, and the process repeated until a drop of the water evaporated to dryness on a slide leaves no residue. The Diatomaceæ then form a white sediment at the bottom of the water, and can be transferred to a slide with a dipping-tube. The drop is then dried with a gentle heat, and the valves mounted as dry transparent objects (p. 12).

If the valves have coarse markings, they may be mounted in balsam; but if the markings are fine, balsam makes them much more difficult of detection.

Many of the most beautiful Diatomaceæ are found in the fossil state; and specimens of these are sold already mounted. I would advise those unacquainted with them to purchase a slide of the "Bermuda" or "Richmond" earth, which abounds in the species of *Coscinodiscus*; and of the "San Fiore deposit," which contains many species of *Epithemia, Navicula, Pinnularia,* &c. These may be procured from Mr. Norman, 178 City Road, or from the microscope-makers.

VOLVOCIN'EÆ.—The Volvocineæ are inhabitants of clear fresh-water pools, on heaths and bogs. They are very minute, of a rounded or plate-like (tabular) form, of a green colour, and are pretty readily distinguished from most of the other Algæ by their free motion; for they swim about in the water like animals, as which they were formerly considered. They consist usually of groups of thick-walled soft cells, each being furnished with one or two cilia, by means of which the movement of the compound bodies is produced.

In the beautiful *Volvox globátor* (which is not uncommon) the cells form a hollow sphere (Pl. VI. fig. 18), studded with exceedingly minute green spots or zoospore-like bodies, representing the green endochrome of the component cells, and from each of which very fine radiating lines extend, so as to give the surface a netted appearance; the lines consisting of delicate processes of the endochrome, which may be compared with those existing in the cells of the hairs of *Tradescantia*. In the interior of the parent globes are often seen several young organisms, usually eight, of a deep green colour; these escape by the rupture of the parent, so as to form independent beings. Sometimes they are found of a yellow colour, and furnished with a thick transparent coat; these are called " resting spores," as they remain for some time before undergoing their full development.

The cilia of *Volvox*, of which there are two to each of the component cells, are difficult to detect; they are best seen when the organism is dried without a cover, or after moistening them with a little solution of iodine, which dyes them brown.

Synúra volvox (Pl. VI. fig. 13) is a still more minute member of this family, and is often found rolling along among *Confervæ*. The greenish zoospore-like bodies of this Alga have one cilium only, and arise from a common centre by a narrowing of the base (fig. 14).

In *Gónium pectoróle* (fig. 11 *a*) the green bodies, which are sixteen in number, and furnished each with two cilia, are grouped into a flat square plate; and in the very minute *Gonium tranquil'lum* (fig. 11 *c*) these bodies are also sixteen in number, and arranged in a tabular form, but are without cilia.

SIPHONA'CEÆ.—The structure of this family may be illustrated by the genus *Vauchéria*, of which two or three species are common on damp ground or in freshwater pools, forming a green layer. At first sight, the filaments of which the little plants consist appear like those of a stout *Conferva*; but on close examination they are found to be branched, and not jointed, consisting of a single cell from end to end (Pl. VI. fig. 26). The reproduction is effected by the agency of two kinds of organs, antheridia and capsules (sporangia), situated near each other (fig. 26 *a*) on the walls of the filaments, of which they are protrusions or outgrowths—their cavities being separated from that of the filament by a partition or septum. The antheridia produce spermatozoa, and the sporangia each a spore, the one fertilizing the other in the ordinary manner. In addition to this method of fructification, zoospores are also produced—the ends of the filaments becoming swollen, the contents cut off by a septum, and forming single large zoospores covered with cilia, the further development of which resembles that occurring in the Confervaceæ.

OSCILLATORIA'CEÆ.—The members of this family are commonly found in stagnant water or on shaded damp ground, especially in the cold seasons of the year, forming green strata or masses.

Oscillatoria autumnális (Pl. VI. fig. 1) occurs everywhere upon damp shaded banks of ditches, espe-

PLATE VI. [PAGE 84.]

FRESHWATER ALGÆ.

Fig.
1. *Oscillatoria autumnalis.*
2. *Oscillatoria nigra.*
3. *Coscinodiscus radiatus.*
4. *Nostoc minutissimum.*
5. *Actinocyclus undulatus.*
6. *Bacterium.*
7. *Rhabdonema arcuatum.*
8. *Rhabdonema arcuatum,* prepared frustules.
9. *Melosira nummuloides.*
10. *Melosira nummuloides,* prepared frustules.
11. *a, b, Gonium pectorale;* 11 *c. Gonium tranquillum.*
12. *Spirulina oscillarioides.*
13. *Synura volvox.*
14. *Synura volvox.*
15. *Gyrosigma attenuatum,* front view.

Fig.
16. *Gyrosigma attenuatum,* side view; 16 *a,* portion of a valve.
17. *Gyrosigma angulatum;* 17 *a,* portion of a valve.
18. *Volvox globator.*
19. *Glæocapsa.*
20. *Chara vulgaris,* globule.
21. *Chara vulgaris,* portion of filament.
22. *Chara vulgaris,* branch with nucule and globule.
23. *Tabellaria flocculosa.*
24. *Tabellaria flocculosa,* prepared frustules.
25. *Palmella cruenta.*
26. *Vaucheria Ungeri (sessilis).*
27. *Vaucheria Ungeri,* capsule.

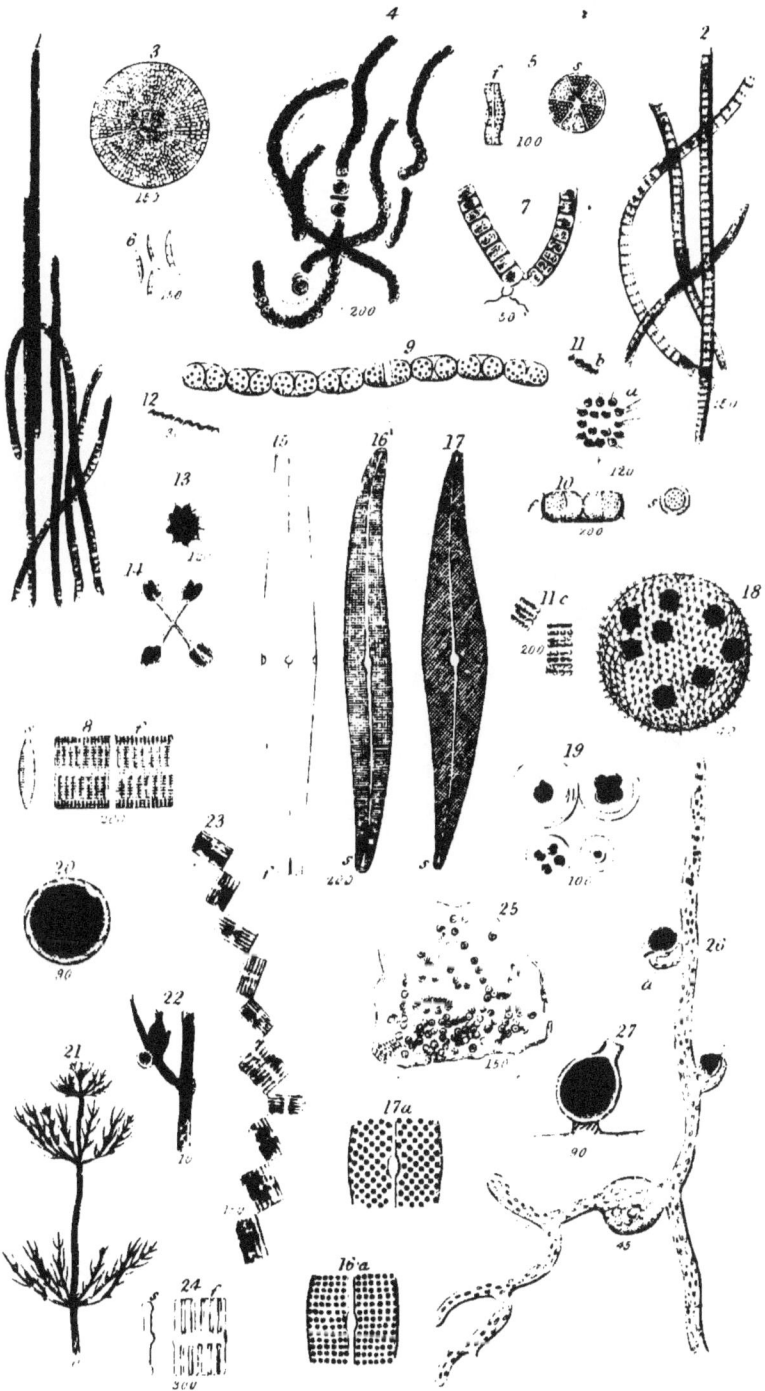

Plate VI.

cially when newly made, forming a greenish-black closely adherent stratum. Under the microscope it is seen to consist of innumerable palish-green filaments; these are jointed or transversely striated, some being straight, others curved, the ends often exhibiting a writhing or worm-like movement. The appearance of these fibres is peculiar, seeming as if they were solid throughout, and so differing from that of the Confervaceæ, in which the cell-walls are readily distinguishable from the cell-contents. The fibres easily break across at the joints; and the last few segments are often narrowed and rounded, so as to form a blunt point. When they have been left in water, they exhibit colourless tubular sheaths surrounding and extending beyond them. These sheaths consist of the consolidated outer portions of the cell-walls; for when the cells undergo transverse division, and expand by growth in the direction of the length of the filament, the original septa or inner walls are broken through, and their remains may often be seen on the inner surface of the sheath, appearing as little teeth.

Oscillatoria nigra (Pl. VI. fig. 2) is another very similar species, forming blackish-green masses, and is common in ditches. It has longer filaments than the last, with narrowed and slightly curved ends; and the endochrome is distinctly granular.

In two other genera of this family, *Vib'rio* and *Spirulína*, the filaments are spiral. *Vib'rio spiril'lum* is excessively minute, colourless, and found in decomposing vegetable mixtures. The short filaments move rapidly through the water, with a corkscrew-like motion. In *Spirulína oscillarioídes* (Pl. VI. fig. 12), which is more rarely found in clear pond-waters among *Confervæ*, the filaments are greenish, and form a beautiful simple spiral, resembling that of a very slender spiral vessel.

Lyng'bya murális (Pl. V. fig. 2) is very common on damp walls, gravel walks, &c. It forms a bright

I

grass-green layer, consisting of somewhat rigid curled filaments. The endochrome is usually broader than long; and the cells of the filaments are often found empty, the endochrome having escaped in the form of gonidia.

Pl. VI. fig. 6 represents a species of *Bactérium* which is not uncommon in decomposing vegetable liquids; the filaments are short, curved, pointed at the ends, and have four joints.

Fig. 26 represents a *Schizogónium*, found upon damp paths. The filaments resemble those of *Lyngbya*, but are united in pairs.

Fig. 3 represents a filament of a *U'lothrix*, which is common in freshwater pools, showing the curious manner in which the endochrome is arranged in the cells, forming bands partially lining the cell-walls.

NOSTOCHA CEÆ.—Two species of the typical genus *Nos'toc* will serve to represent this family. *Nos'toc commúne* is found on damp ground or in ponds, and forms to the naked eye firmish, olive-green, skin-like, plaited masses, an inch or more in diameter. Under the microscope it is seen to consist of numerous beaded fibres, imbedded in worm-like gelatinous sheaths; these are curved and interwoven to form the compound mass. In the middle of many of the filaments is an enlarged colourless cell, called the vesicular cell, which is related to the reproduction, but in a manner not yet determined.

Nostoc minutis'simum (Pl. VI. fig. 4) forms solid gelatinous bluish-green masses, varying in size from a pin's head to a pea; it is found upon unhealthy water-plants kept in glass vessels. The component filaments are very slender, wavy, and the sheaths often have a brownish tinge.

ULVACEÆ.—These Algæ are mostly marine—some, however, being found in brackish or fresh water, or on damp ground, thatch, moss, &c. They are generally of considerable size, forming flat or tubular

fronds, often several inches long, a few being filamentous. They consist of one or more sheets or
layers of cells, containing mostly green endochrome.
This at first fills the cells, but subsequently becomes
converted into single spores, or subdivided into numerous ciliated zoospores.

Ul'va latis'sima is very common on the sea-coast,
being found attached to stones, shells, &c. It forms
a broad, flat, green, rounded or ̮oblong, thin frond,
wavy and crumpled at the margins, and from 6 to
18 inches in length. The minute cells form two
layers, adherent to each other. The zoospores formed
are numerous in each cell.

Enteromor'pha compres'sa (Pl. IV. fig. 31) is also
common in the sea and in brackish ditches; it is
often found floating. The frond is green, tubular,
flattened or compressed, and branched, the branches
being usually simple and narrowed at the base. The
frond consists of two layers of minute cells, separated
by a space rendering it hollow. The zoospores are
numerous in the cells (fig. 32).

PALMELLA'CEÆ.—These Algæ are found in fresh or
salt water, or on damp earth, wood, &c. They are
green or red, forming round or irregular masses or
strata. They consist of loosely connected cells, imbedded in a gelatinous mass or matrix, thus forming
a frond.

Chlorococ'cum vulgáre (Pl. II. fig.1) is very common
upon the bark of elm-trees, palings, &c., forming a
green granular crust. It consists of minute rounded
or oval cells, mostly undergoing division into twos,
fours, or eights. These cells are attached to the
sides or ends of very fine colourless filaments. It is
most probable that this organism, which is usually
placed among the Algæ, consists of the gonidia of a
Lichen.

Chlorococcum muror'um forms a somewhat similar
but soft and thin green layer, upon damp walls or

other porous bodies. It consists of very minute oval green cells, with thick walls, and imbedded in the ends of prolongations of a gelatinous matrix.

Palmel'la cruen'ta (Pl. VI. fig. 25) forms a portwine-red layer at the bottom of damp walls or on the ground. It is composed of pale red cells, imbedded in no definite order in a colourless gelatinous matrix. The cells are filled with red granules, and are often found undergoing division.

Pl. VI. fig. 19 represents a species of *Glæocap'sa*, in which the cell-envelopes do not soften and unite to form a gelatinous matrix, as in *Palmella* and other members of the family, but are persistent.   This species occurs in fresh water containing Confervæ.

CHARA'CEÆ.—This family consists of the single genus *Chára*, the systematic position of which is not agreed upon by authors; as however its structure will be better understood after what has been gone over, it may be conveniently considered here.

There are several species of *Chara*, the one illustrated, *Chara vulgáris* (Pl. VI. fig. 21), being commonly found in ditches and pools. It consists of long main stems, often a foot in length, which are branched, and surrounded at tolerably regular intervals by whorls of branchlets. In some species, the stems and branches consist simply of elongated cells, arranged end to end ; while in others, of which *Chara vulgaris* is one, the central cells are surrounded by a number of narrower spirally arranged cells, forming an outer coating.

The Charæ have long formed interesting microscopic objects, on account of the circulation of the protoplasm being visible in the cells, as in the hairs of *Tradescantia*. This is best seen in those species in which the outer layer of cells is absent from the stems, and which were formerly arranged in a separate genus (*Nitella*). But it may also be seen in the stems and especially the young branchlets of any of the other species ; and as the granules of the protoplasm are large, the phenomenon is more easily witnessed than in *Tradescantia*.

The fructification consists of two kinds of organs, viz. red *globules* (Pl. VI. fig. 22) representing the anther-organ, and green capsules (fig. 22), or *nucules*, corresponding to the ovaries. The structure of the globules is very curious. Their transparent walls (fig. 20) consist of eight somewhat triangular plates, each of which is composed of cells radiating from a centre; and from the inside of each of these centres arises a tubular cell extending to the middle of the globule, the unattached ends giving origin to numerous colourless coiled filaments, consisting of minute cells arranged end to end, each containing a very minute coiled spiral fibre, to which are attached two exceedingly slender cilia. These ciliated fibres are the spermatozoa. The capsules or nucules (fig. 22), which are situated near the globules, are urn-shaped, coated with spiral cells, and crowned with five shorter cells. When the globules are ripe, they become ruptured by the separation of the valves; and the spermatozoa, escaping from the cells of the coiled filaments, swim about and enter a canal in the capsules to fertilize the ovule contained within.

The *Charæ* grow readily in a glass jar of fresh water, with a few pebbles at the bottom; and if the plants be not overgrown with Confervoids, the fructification will continue to be produced almost throughout the year.

The circulation is best seen in the whorled branchlets, a portion of the growing ends being placed in a live-box, or simply laid upon a slide in water and covered with thin glass.

Preservation.—The Algæ are best preserved in two ways,—the entire fronds being dried upon paper under pressure, as directed for the Ferns; and small portions, showing the minuter structures and fructification, being mounted in chloride of calcium or glycerine. If it is required to preserve the marine Algæ according to the first method, they should first be immersed for a time in fresh water, to dissolve out the saline matters derived from the sea-water, which would keep them damp and ultimately spoil them. After these matters have been removed, the fresh water should be changed, and pieces of paper placed beneath them while suspended in the water; on withdrawing the paper carefully, keeping the Algæ at the same time spread out, they may be made to retain the required position; and when the water has drained away, and the remaining moisture has mostly evaporated, they may be submitted to pressure in a press.

The Confervoid Algæ may be conveniently spread out upon paper and preserved in the same manner, as some of the distinguishing characters are founded upon their appearance in the dry state, their adhesion to the paper, &c. Moreover they can then at any time be minutely examined, by the immersion of a small portion in water.

CHAPTER VIII.

LICHENS.

THE Lichens are found growing upon the bark of trees, old palings, &c. Those most easily seen with the naked eye form grey or coloured dryish patches or pendulous tufts; while the smaller ones are singly easily overlooked, from their minute size and close adhesion to the *mátrix* or body upon which they grow, forming, by their aggregation, the grey or otherwise-coloured dry and brittle coatings of almost every tree or decaying branch.

The Lichens derive their nourishment from the air, and not from the matrix—in this respect differing from the Fungi, with some of which, as we shall presently see, they agree in the structure of the fruit.

The structure of the Lichens is simple, no distinction of root, stem, and leaves existing in them, although certain dry root-like fibres exist in many of them, by which the plant is fixed to the matrix. The whole consists mainly of a frond or *thal'lus* ($\theta\alpha\lambda\lambda\grave{o}\varsigma$, a leaf). This is either raised above the surface of the matrix in a shrubby form, or spread upon the surface as a flexible lobed layer (Pl. II. fig. 2), or it is dry and brittle (crustaceous) and closely adherent (Pl. II. fig. 26).

The fructification consists of little saucers, disks, or streak-like furrows, often of a different colour from the thallus, the structure of which will be best illustrated by reference to a few common species.

PARMELIA'CEÆ.—*Parmélia parietína* (Pl. II. fig. 2) is a very common Lichen, found on the bark of trees, on old palings, &c. It is of an orange-yellow colour, the thallus being flat, lobed, and scalloped (crenate) at the margins. The structure of the thallus may serve to represent that of most of the Lichens. It consists of three layers,—an upper cortical or epidermic layer, which is continued over the margins to the under surface of the thallus, to form the under layer; and between these is the middle or medullary layer. The medullary layer consists of interwoven fibres, which are more closely packed towards the upper and under surfaces, so as to give them a cellular appearance. Near the upper part of the medullary layer, a number of minute rounded green cells exist, lying loosely in its meshes (Pl. II. fig. 4 *a*). These green cells (gonidia) appear to correspond to the buds of the higher plants, and, when detached from the plants, they are capable of growing into new individuals.

On the upper surface of the thallus of *Parmelia* (fig. 2) the fructification may be observed. This consists of saucers or shields (*apothécia*, ἀποθήκη, a repository), formed of a raised and expanded portion of the thallus (fig. 3), and containing the spores. The spores are enclosed in closely set upright cells, or spore-sacs (figs. 4 *b* and 5 *b*), called *as'ci* (ἀσκὸς, a bottle) or thecæ; and intermingled with the asci are filaments, enlarged and coloured at the ends (*paraphyses*), which are probably abortive asci.

In systematic works upon the Lichens, the saucers and their contents are included in the term apothecia, the saucer alone being called the *excip'ulum* (*excipulum*, a receiver); the mass of asci and paraphyses forming the *nucleus* or *thalámium* (θάλαμος, a bed).

The yellow spores are very minute, each ascus containing eight of them, and they are divided by a transverse partition or septum.

Near the margins of the lobes of the thallus are small dark points. These are the pouting mouths of little capsules (*spermogonia*) sunk in the substance of the thallus, and containing numerous filaments, terminated by very minute stick-shaped bodies (*spermatia*), which break off and escape through the orifices of the capsules. These are probably the representatives of the anthers of flowering plants and of the antheridia of the ferns. They are, however, so difficult to find and examine, that I must refer to the Dictionary for a further description and figures of them.

LECIDIN'EÆ. — This family contains the genus *Cladónia*, three or four species of which are common on boggy heaths, banks, &c., viz. *Cladonia coccif'era*, the Scarlet Cup-moss (Pl. II. fig. 21); *C. pyxidáta*, the Common Cup-moss (Pl. II. fig. 23); *C. vermiculáris* (Pl. II. fig. 22); and *C. rangiferína*, the Reindeer Moss (Pl. II. fig. 24). The thallus of these Lichens forms little rounded irregularly overlapping scales, with scalloped edges, overgrowing the surface upon which the Lichens are found. The fruit-stalks, or *podétia* (πούς, a foot), are hollow (fistulose), and either simple and dilated into cups (Pl. II. fig. 23), or branched with the corners or angles between the adjacent branches perforated. The apothecia in the young state resemble those of *Parmelia* on a small scale; but as they approach maturity, the centre becomes pushed up, so that the spore-layer is extended over the ends of the stalks. In *C. coccifera* and *pyxidata* the cups are proliferous at the margin; *i. e.*, branches upon which the apothecia are placed arise from it. The asci and paraphyses are very minute, but do not differ essentially in structure from those of *Parmelia*. In *C. vermicularis* the podetia are pointed and more solid than in the other species, the apothecia forming very minute spots at their apices.

GRAPHID'EÆ. — To this family belong *Gráphis scripta* (Pl. II. fig. 26) and *Opeg'rapha betulína* (Pl. II. fig. 30). These little Lichens are easily overlooked, from the thin and but slightly raised thallus being only visible to the naked eye as a discoloration of the bark

of the trees upon which they grow; while the fructification is very minute, forming little black streaks
or *lirel'læ* (*lira*, a furrow), irregularly arranged, and
resembling somewhat the letters of some of the Ori-
ental alphabets.

In *Graphis scripta* (fig. 26) the thallus is thin,
somewhat membranous, smoothish, shining, greyish
white, and faintly bordered with black. The lirellæ
(fig. 27) are partly sunk in the bark, winding and
narrow, some being simple, others branched; and
they are surrounded by a raised border, formed by
the thallus. The lirellæ are lined at the sides with
a black (carbonaceous) layer or *excip'ulum*, within
which are situated the asci and paraphyses. The
spores (Pl. II. fig. 29) are 8-cleft, the segments being
again divided longitudinally into little spores or
sporidia.

In *Opegrapha betulina* (Pl. II. fig. 30), which is
found on the bark of the birch-tree, the thallus is
thin, dirty yellowish white, bordered with black. The
lirellæ (figs. 31, 32) are mostly simple, without a
raised border of the thallus, and the excipulum forms
a complete lining to them. The spores (fig. 33 *a*) are
3-cleft, and taper at the ends.

CALICI'EÆ.—*Calic'ium clavel'lum* (Pl. II. fig. 6) is
a pretty little Lichen, growing upon old boards and
farm-buildings. The thallus is granular and greyish
white. The apothecia (fig. 7) are stalked and black,
but of a lighter colour than the mass of spores forming the nucleus. The spores are very minute, black,
oblong, and divided by a transverse septum.

The Lichens are divided into two Orders, according
to whether the apothecia are open before the spores
are ripe, as in the species noticed above, or whether
the apothecia only open to discharge the ripe spores.
The first Order forms the *Gymnocar'pi* (γυμνὸς, naked,
καρπὸς, fruit); the second forms the *Angiocar'pi* (ἀγ-
γεῖον, vessel, capsule).

Preservation.—The Lichens are readily preserved, on account of their dry nature; they need simply be kept in a dry place, and glued to pieces of card. If room is an object, they may be dried under pressure, as in the case of the flowering plants. When remoistened, the minute structures may be easily made out by sections. The smaller ones may be mounted dry, in cells made of the wax cement (p. 16). The minute structures keep well in chloride of calcium or glycerine.

CHAPTER IX.

FUNGI.

THE Fungi form the lowest class of plants: as examples of them, may be mentioned mushrooms, toadstools, puff-balls, the mould of paste, the blue mould
of cheese, &c. The more minute Fungi are very
common, forming beautiful microscopic objects, although they are rarely studied by the microscopic
observer.

Fungi live usually upon rotting or decaying vegetable substances, as rotten wood, the dead leaves and
stems of plants, &c.; but sometimes they are found
upon living plants, and some of them exist upon decaying animal matters, and even in living animals.

Fungi exhibit no separation of root, stem, or leaves,
as exists in the higher plants; nor do they contain
chlorophyll, the presence of which is so generally
associated with the idea of a plant. But they consist
of aggregations of mostly elongate cells, forming
branched and interlacing colourless fibres, buried like
roots in the substance (matrix) upon which they grow,
and from which they derive their nourishment; this
portion of the Fungus is called the *mycélium* (μύκης,
a fungus). The portion of the Fungus projecting
beyond the surface of the matrix is the fructification;
and this is the part usually called the fungus, the
mycelium being overlooked by a casual observer. So
that here we have a character distinguishing the
Fungi from the Lichens, which derive their nourishment from the air, and not from the matrix. The
absence of the green cells, or gonidia, forms another

PLATE VII.   [PAGE 96.]

FUNGI.

Fig.
1. *Agaricus micaceus* : *a,* gills.
2. *Agaricus campestris* : *a,* spores ; *b,* basidia.
3. *Physarum album,* on a piece of stick.
4. *Physarum album,* spores.
5. *Uredo segetum,* spores.
6. *Uredo caries,* spores.
7. *Uredo candida,* on leaf of Shepherd's Purse(*Capsella*): *s,* spores.
8. *Æcidium grossulariæ,* sorus.
9. *Æcidium grossulariæ* : *p,* sporecapsules (peridia): *s,* anthercapsules (spermogonia).
10. *Nemaspora crocea* : *a,* spores.
11. *Torula casei.*
12. *Torula herbarum,* on a piece of stick.
13. *Torula herbarum,* spores.
14. *Phragmidium bulbosum,* on bramble-leaf.
15. *Phragmidium bulbosum,* stylospores and paraphyses.
16. *Puccinia graminis,* on a piece of straw.

Fig.
17. *Puccinia graminis,* spores.
18. *Sporocybe alternata,* filament and spores.
19. *Botrytis parasitica,* on Shepherd's Purse.
20. *Botrytis parasitica,* spores and filaments.
21. *Rhinotrichum,* species of.
22. *Rhinotrichum,* heads of spores.
23. *Rhinotrichum,* spores detached.
24. *Rhinotrichum,* spores.
25. *Penicillium glaucum.*
26. *Penicillium glaucum,* head of spores.
27. *Coremium leucopus.*
28. *Tubercularia vulgaris.*
29. *Tubercularia vulgaris,* divided receptacle.
30. *Tubercularia vulgaris,* filaments.
31. *Tubercularia vulgaris,* spores.
32. *Sphæria fragiformis.*
33. *Trichothecium roseum,* on a piece of stick.
34. *Trichothecium roseum.*
35. *Trichothecium roseum,* filaments and spores.

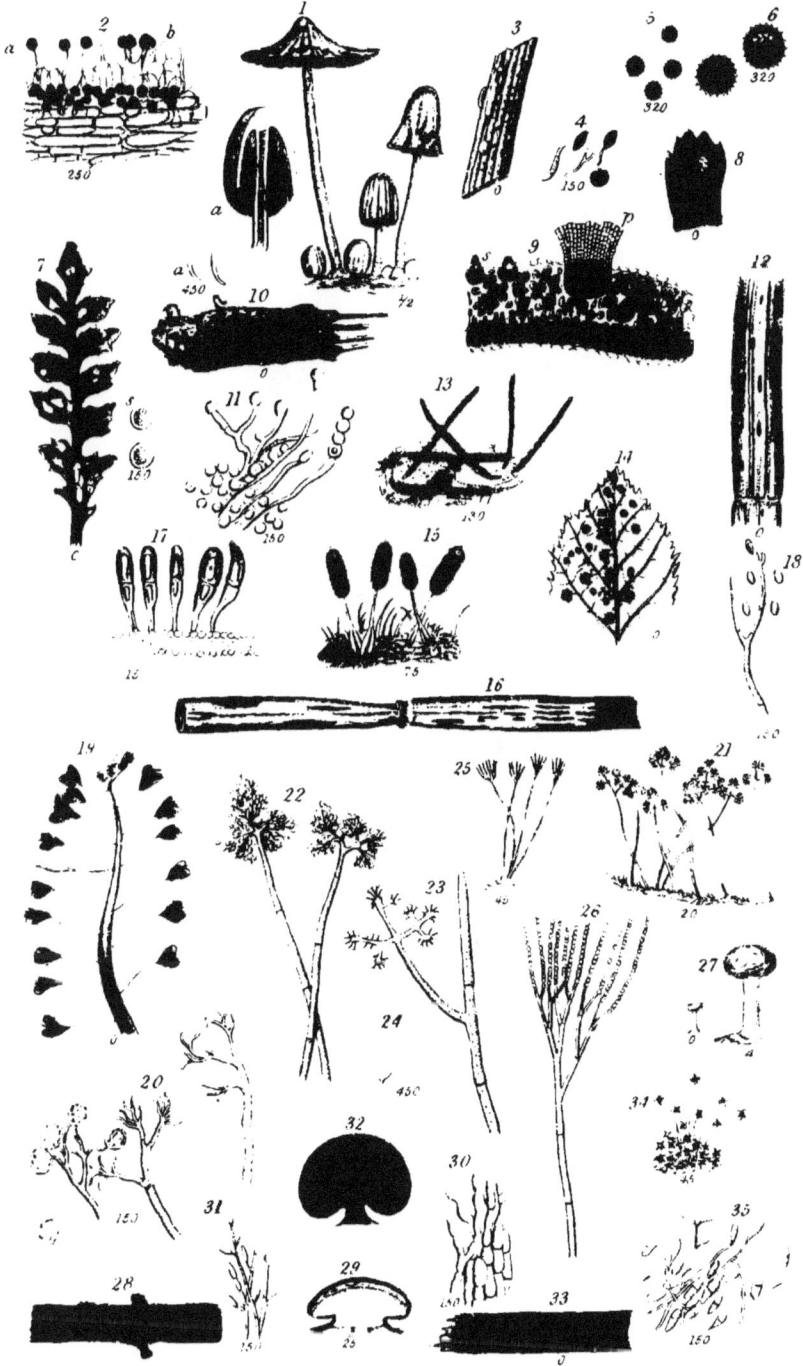

Plate VII

character by which the nearly allied members of this class of plants can be distinguished.

The fructification of the Fungi occurs in two distinct forms, in one of which the seeds or spores are naked, and situated at the ends of slender cells or filaments, whilst in the other the spores are contained in usually flask-like cells, called asci, similar to those occurring in the Lichens. In a few Fungi, antheridial organs, called spermogonia, as in the case of the Lichens, have also been detected. The Fungi are divided into six Orders, from each of which a few species may be selected to illustrate their structure more in detail.

HYMENOMYCE'TES ($\dot{v}\mu\dot{\eta}\nu$, membrane, $\mu\dot{v}\kappa\eta\varsigma$, fungus). This is the highest Order of Fungi, containing a large number of genera and species; as examples of which may be mentioned the common Mushroom, Toadstools, &c.

Their general structure may be illustrated by the examination of the common Mushroom (*Agar'icus campes'tris*); the species figured (Pl. VII. fig. 1), however, being *Agaricus micáceus*, which is common at the root of trees, the bottom of decaying posts, &c.

The vegetative part of the fungus consists of a cotton-like mycelium, which is composed of slender, colourless, interwoven filaments, popularly known as the spawn. The portion commonly called the mushroom corresponds to the fructification, and consists of certain parts visible to the naked eye. These are an expanded portion at the top, forming a hemispherical cap, receptacle, or *píleus* (*pileus*, a cap), and a stalk, or *stipes*, upon which the cap is supported. On the under surface of the cap are a number of nearly parallel, radiating, dark-coloured plates or *gills*, somewhat resembling the gill-plates of a fish. The dark colour of the gills arises from the presence of the spores, which are coloured, although in some species they are white. The surface of the gills, upon

K

caying stems, sticks, &c. The mycelium consists of inconspicuous, fine filaments, which run beneath the epidermis and bark of leaves and stems, or exist in the intercellular passages, the fruit bursting through the surface. The spores are short-stalked, forming *sty'lospores* (στῦλος, stalk, σπόρος, seed) or *conid'ia* (κονίδιον, little dust). But there is great confusion in the descriptions of the spores of the same Fungus by different botanical authors, some describing the fruit (in Pl. VII. fig. 15, for instance) as composed of rows of spores, while others regard it as forming a single septate (*septum*, a partition) or partitioned spore.

Tor'ula herbárum (Pl. VII. fig. 12) is very common on the decaying stems of plants, especially those belonging to the Parsley order (Umbelliferæ), forming greenish-black streaks or patches. The spores (fig. 13) are grouped into chains or beaded (moniliform) rows, with very short stalks, and these are crowded to form the black patches visible to the naked eye. Under the microscope the spores appear of a brown colour.

Torula cásei (Pl. VII. fig. 11) forms reddish or white patches upon decaying cheese. It consists of branched, interwoven, tufted filaments (*flocci*), with comparatively large spherical spores arranged in rows at their ends.

Nemas'pora crócea (Pl. VII. fig. 10) is a very curious member of this Order, and is found upon decaying beech-sticks. It appears as an orange-coloured tendril-like gelatinous mass of spores, bursting through a little pore on the surface of the bark. The spores (fig. 10 a) are very minute, slender, and curved, and under a high power appear jointed.

Æcid'ium grossuláriæ (Pl. VII. fig. 8) is found very commonly on the leaves of the gooseberry-bush. It forms to the naked eye oval or rounded spots (*sori*), of a red colour; and on close examination, the spots appear dotted with yellow points. Each point is the rifice of an open capsule (*peridium*), which has burst through the epidermis of the leaf (Pl. VII. fig. 9 *p*). The capsules are split or lacerated at the margins, and form little cups containing the spores. The spores are very minute, yellow, and are arranged in closely packed moniliform rows. The red colour depends upon the altered chlorophyll of the leaf. On the leaves containing the spore-capsules or peridia will be found smaller, brownish-yellow capsules (*spermogonia*) partly imbedded in their substance (Pl. VII. fig. 9 *s*). These contain minute filaments (*sterigmata*), terminated by short rows of rounded cells (*spermatia*), which are supposed to exert an antheridial function. The species of *Æcidium* are very numerous, and many of them are extremely common—as those upon the nettle, the barberry, the dandelion, the wood-anemone, the violet, and buttercups. The groups of capsules form exquisite opake objects under a low power of the microscope.

Phragmid'ium bulbósum (Pl. VII. fig. 14) is another very beautiful coniomycetous Fungus. It forms little reddish, afterwards sooty dots upon the under surface of the leaves of various species of Bramble (*Rúbus*). The oblong spores (fig. 15) are from 2- to 4-septate, and stalked, the stalks being swollen or bulbous at the base. The spores, which appear brown when magnified, are covered with little knobs (tuberculate) on the surface; and the uppermost little spore or sporidium is terminated by a minute point (apiculate). Among the spores are numerous barren filaments or paraphyses.

Puccin'ia gram'inis (Pl. VII. fig. 16) is to be found everywhere upon damp rotting straw, and upon grasses. It forms sooty irregular streaks, consisting of densely crowded, one-partitioned (uniseptate) spores (fig. 17), which appear brown under the microscope. This Fungus is sometimes called "mildew." There are numerous other species of *Puccinia* which occur upon common plants.

Urédo seg'etum is the " smut" of wheat, barley, and oats—a fungus too well known to the farmer. It forms sooty masses, bursting through the epidermis of the stalk and ears of the corn, and soiling the fingers when handled. The spores (Pl. VII. fig. 5) are exceedingly minute, and the stalks are so slender and loosely connected with them that they are not readily detected. Under the microscope the spores appear brown and faintly dotted, this appearance arising from a reticulated structure of the surface, similar to that of the poppy-seed on a very small scale.

Urédo cáries is the " bunt" of corn. It grows within the grain, filling it with a sooty, fœtid mass. The spores (Pl. VII. fig. 6) are considerably larger than those of the last species, and their surface is distinctly reticulated. They are attached to the filaments of the mycelium, as in *Uredo segetum*.

The spores of both these species of *Uredo* may be found in most kinds of flour and bread, especially in those of inferior quality.

Urédo can'dida (Pl. VII. fig. 7) is another species, forming white dots upon the leaves of the common Shepherd's Purse (*Capsel'la bur'sa pastor'is*)—which is easily recognized by the form and arrangement of the pods (fig. 19). The spores (*s*) are rather large and white.

Other species of *Uredo* are very common upon numerous species of weeds or wild flowering plants; and they so closely resemble each other that, when one is known, the others are easily recognized. Usually each species occurs upon a distinct species of plant, as is the case with parasites generally. In many of them the spots (*sori*) exhibit a thin membrane covering the spores, which bursts down the middle, so as to bear some resemblance to a capsule. But there is no true capsule, the membrane consisting of the epidermis of the leaf or stalk of the plant, which is raised and torn by the expansion of the growing fungus; so that the peridium is spurious, as belonging to the matrix, and not to the fungus. It may be mentioned here that the so-called species of *Uredo* are not truly distinct species, but are the forms of species of *Puccinia, Phragmidium,* &c.; so that the latter genera have two kinds of fruit, one of which is a *Uredo,* the other a *Puccinia.* But I must refer to the Dictionary for further details upon this point.

HYPHOMYCE'TES (ὑφάω, to weave, μύκης, fungus). In this, the 4th Order of Fungi, are contained many of the commonest moulds which are found growing upon decaying substances, and sometimes upon living plants. The mycelium creeps among the particles of the substance, or the elements of the tissues, upon which the Fungus lives, in the form of slender threads or filaments. The spores, which are either simple or partitioned (septate), and naked, occur either singly or in rows at the ends of fine interwoven cottony threads or *floc'ci* (*floc'cus,* a flock of wool), which are generally very evident to the naked eye. The threads supporting the spores form the *ped'icels* (*pedicel'lus,* a little foot). In technical descriptions, these filaments, which are usually composed of cells arranged end to end, are said to be *septate* (Pl. VII. fig. 26), and not jointed, as in the case of the filaments of the *Confervæ,* which are constructed in a similar manner. When not septate, the filaments are said to be *continuous.*

STILBA'CEI.—To this family belongs *Tuberculária vulgaris* (Pl. VII. fig. 28), which is found upon decaying sticks and branches of trees, especially the lime-tree. It forms little firm red knobs or tubercles, each of which is a receptacle. On making a section of a receptacle (Pl. VII. fig. 29), the interior is seen to be paler than the bright red surface, and a short broad stalk comes into view. The receptacle is composed of crowded cell-filaments, so short near the base as rather to resemble cellular tissue (fig. 30); but

towards the surface the filaments become extremely
slender and branched ; and each branch is terminated
by a minute oblong spore, or a short row of them
(fig. 31).

If a stick with this Fungus upon it be kept for some
time in a damp place, short whitish fibres, branched
at the ends, and visible to the naked eye, will be seen
sprouting from around the base of the receptacle
(Pl. VIII. fig. 1). These, when examined under the
microscope, appear composed of fine filaments (Pl.
VIII. fig. 2), resembling those of *Tubercularia*, and
having the minute spores at the ends. After a considerable time, the entire receptacle of the *Tubercularia* becomes resolved into these fibres. In this
state the Fungus assumes the characters of an *Isária*,
a genus of a different family of Fungi (*Isariacei*), so
that we have here an *Isaria*-form of *Tubercularia*.

Sometimes the tubercles of the *Tubercularia* become darker, almost black, harder, and granular on the
surface. On making a section of them in this state,
the whole of the under portion of the surface is found
to contain little roundish capsules, containing asci
and spores, and it constitutes *Sphæ'ria fragifor'mis* (Pl.
VII. fig. 32). As the *Sphæria* is the more complex
and highly organized condition of this Fungus, the
other two conditions must be regarded as forms, and
not as species of separate genera.

DEMATIE'I.—In this family the filaments upon
which the spores are placed are not compacted as in
Tubercularia, but separate; and they are of a dark
brown or black colour.

Sporoc'ybe alternáta (Pl. VII. fig. 18) is occasionally found upon decaying vegetable substances, forming little black velvety spots or patches. The mycelial filaments are exceedingly minute, septate, tapering at the ends, and terminated by a little tuft of
pear-shaped cells, from which the black simple spores
arise singly.

PLATE VIII. [PAGE 104.]

FUNGI.

Fig.

1. *Isaria*-form of *Tubercularia*.
2. *Isaria*-form of *Tubercularia*, filaments.
3. *Aspergillus glaucus*.
4. *Aspergillus glaucus*, filaments and heads of spores; *a*, separate spores.
5. *Aspergillus glaucus*, head of spores.
6. *Peziza omphalodes*.
7. *Peziza stercorea*.
8. *Peziza stercorea*, cup (receptacle).
9. *Peziza stercorea*, asci and paraphyses.
10. *Peziza stercorea*, divided receptacle.
11. *Peziza stercorea*, bristles.
12. *Dothidea typhina*, on leaf-stalk of grass.
13. *Dothidea typhina*, surface of patch (stroma).
14. *Dothidea typhina*, capsules (perithecia).
15. *Dothidea typhina*, ascus containing spores.
16. *Sphæria rubella*, on nettle-stem.
17. *Sphæria rubella*, asci.
18. *Sphæria rubella*, capsules (perithecia).
19. *Sphæria rubella*, ascus and spores.
20. *Sphæria bullata*, on piece of stick;

Fig.

20 *a*, section of tubercle (receptacle).
21. *Sphæria bullata*, asci and spores.
22. *Sphæria complanata*, on piece of stick.
23. *Sphæria complanata*, tubercles (receptacles).
24. *Dothidea ulmi*, on elm-leaf.
25. *Dothidea ulmi*, asci.
26. *Dothidea ulmi*, section of receptacle.
27. *Dothidea ulmi*, spores.
28. *Chætomium elatum*; 28 *a*, spores; 28 *b*, filaments.
29. *Chætomium elatum*, on piece of stick.
30. *Hysterium fraxini*, on piece of stick.
31. *Hysterium fraxini*, receptacle.
32. *Hysterium fraxini*, ascus with spores.
33. *Erysiphe guttata*, on hazel-leaf.
34. *Erysiphe guttata*, capsule.
35. *Erysiphe guttata*, capsule (conceptacle) with fulcra.
36. *Mucor mucedo*: *a*, columella; *s*, spores.
37. *Acrostalagmus*: *a*, spores.
38. Gall on oak-leaf.
39. Gall on oak-leaf.

Muced'ines.—Many of the Fungi belonging to this family are extremely common on decaying vegetable substances, and some are found upon living plants, to which they are very injurious. To the naked eye they usually appear as mouldy or cottony masses, either white, black, or coloured blue, yellow, &c. The spores are attached singly or in rows to branchlets arising from the ends of the filaments, so as to form little heads.

Bot'rytis parasit'ica (Pl. VII. fig. 19) is common upon the flower-stalks of the Shepherd's Purse, forming white mealy patches. The fruit-stalks are comparatively large and thin-walled, the branchlets being slender, mostly curved, and terminated each by a large, spherical, smooth, simple, white spore.

Botrytis vulgáris is also common on various decaying plants. Its filaments are grey, and the branchlets lobe-like; the spores being minute, spherical, either white or greenish, and placed simply at the tips.

Botrytis infes'tans is the potato-Fungus. It forms white spots upon the under side of the leaves of the potato-plant, and by some authors is considered to be the cause of the potato-disease. The filaments are branched at the ends, and terminated by single oval spores, which are apiculate at the free end, and contain minute little spores or sporidia.

Oid'ium Tuck'eri is the well-known destructive grape-Fungus. It forms white cottony masses upon the vine and its grapes, the fruit-stalks being short and terminated by one or two end-to-end oblong spores. It appears to be the Coniomycetous form of another Fungus (*Erysiphe*).

Trichothécium róseum (Pl. VII. fig. 33) is found upon rotting sticks; very frequently upon willow-baskets kept in a damp place. It forms little rounded, slightly raised, pinkish spots, less than the size of a pin's head. The branched and septate foot-stalks (figs. 34, 35) are terminated each by a little group of obovate spores, divided by a transverse partition (uni-septate). Sometimes this little Fungus is quite white, at others greenish; when perfectly ripe, the spores become oblong.

Penicil'lium glaúcum (Pl. VII. fig. 25) is the common Blue Mould found upon decaying substances, as cheese, &c., the interwoven mycelial filaments often forming large cakes or crusts upon the surface. The septate fruit-stalks (fig. 26) are fork-branched at the ends, the branchlets being terminated each by a row of very minute spherical smooth spores. On some decaying substances, as apples, gum, &c., the fruit-stalks are found aggregated into a thick stalk, the branchlets and spores forming a rounded head, so that the whole resembles a little blue mushroom (fig. 27). In this form the Fungus has been placed in a distinct genus, and called *Corémium leúcopus.* In other species the spores are pink and white.

This little Fungus is of special interest, on account of one form of it constituting the yeast-plant, or yeast as it is commonly called. This consists of rounded or oblong cells, which grow very rapidly in fermenting liquids by budding—the large quantity of sugar and gluten present favouring the vegetative or simple growing process, at the expense of the fructifying process. But this is only an instance of what we constantly find in flowering plants, the use of very rich soil rendering flowers double, which is really reducing their organs to the state of leaves. When the sugar has become exhausted, the cells of the yeast become longer and thinner, as if starved; they then form a more recognizable mycelium, which extends to the surface of the liquid, and produces finally the fruit-stalks and the *Penicillium* fruit.

Aspergil'lus glaúcus (Pl. VIII. fig. 3) is an extremely common mould upon cheese, jams, &c. It resembles the last in appearance to the naked eye, except that it has rather a green tinge, the heads of fruit being much more compact and rounded. The fruit-stalks (fig. 4) are large, bulbous or inflated at the ends (fig. 5), and from the inflations arise the crowded rows of spores. The spores are rounded, and rough (scabrous) on the surface. On removing most of the spores from the head of fruit, each row of spores is found to arise from a very short stalk.

Plate VII. fig. 21 represents a beautiful species of *Rhinot'richum*, which is found upon decaying and sickly plants, and upon rotting sticks, forming a minute grey mould. The fruit-stalks (fig. 22) are large, sparingly branched, septate or jointed, appearing brownish under the microscope. Their ends are branched, mostly biternate (fig. 23), *i. e.* each branch dividing into three branchlets, and these again into three still finer ones. The ends of the branchlets are inflated, and coated with little points, upon each of which a smooth white spore (fig. 24) is placed.

ASCOMYCÉTES (ἀσκὸς, a bottle, μύκης, fungus). The Fungi belonging to this Order are found upon the stems and leaves of plants, and upon decaying substances, as dung, &c. They are usually evident to the naked eye, some even equalling the Hymenomycetous Fungi in size; and many of them are brilliantly coloured. They are in general distinguishable with facility from the Fungi of other Orders, by the arrangement of the spores in colourless sacs or asci (Pl. VIII. fig. 9), resembling those noticed in the case of the Lichens. These asci are usually enclosed in a capsule or *perithécium*. The mycelium is usually buried in the matrix, so as not to be conspicuous.

Helvellácei.—To this family belongs the large genus *Peziza*, some of the species of which are beautifully coloured, yet scarcely microscopic. Among these may be mentioned *Peziza omphalódes* (Pl. VIII. fig. 6), which forms little red masses upon damp ceilings. It does not possess the ordinary form of a *Peziza*, which is that of a cup fixed at the end of a stalk, like a mushroom with the cup turned inside out, the asci lining its interior.

Peziza coccin'ea is not uncommon in woods. It is whitish outside, the interior of the cup being of a brilliant scarlet colour. It is from half an inch to an inch in height.

Peziza stercor'ea (Pl. VIII. fig. 7) is often found upon dung. The surface of the cup of this Fungus is granular and covered with bristles (figs. 8 & 11). The cup is concave (fig. 10), and lined with the asci (fig. 9), among which are simple paraphyses.

The *Pezizæ* are excellent Ascomycetous Fungi for exhibiting the asci, as they are more or less soft, and thus sections of them may be easily prepared, or they may readily be picked to pieces with the mounted needles.

TUBERACEI.—In this family is contained the Truffle (*Túber cibárium*). The asci are situated upon the inner surfaces of the winding canals traversing the substance of the fleshy fruit (*peridium*) of which the truffle consists.

PHACIDIA'CEI.—To this family belongs *Hystérium frax'ini* (Pl. VIII. fig. 30), which is found upon ash-twigs. The drawn-out capsules or perithecia (fig. 31) are black and elliptical, with a longitudinal fissure or orifice, and contain the asci (fig. 32) with the spores.

SPHÆRIÁCEI.—*Dothid'ea typhína* (Pl. VIII. fig. 12) is a common Fungus upon the stems of living grasses. It forms an orange-coloured patch or layer encircling the stem, and covered with little dots. On making a section (fig. 14), it appears composed of a row of oblong or obovate closely placed capsules (perithecia) immersed in and continuous with a finely fibrous receptacular mass (*stróma*). The asci (fig. 15) are very slender, arising in a tuft from the bottom of the capsules, and containing eight still more slender spores. Except under a very high power, the spores appear as interrupted lines running down the interior of the asci. The little dots visible to the naked eye are the slightly projecting mouths of the capsules, which are more distinctly seen in the magnified portion of the Fungus (fig. 13). In the young state, this Fungus is whitish.

This Fungus cannot be mistaken for a *Uredo*, two species of which occur upon grasses—*Uredo lineáris* forming yellowish-brown spots, and *Uredo rubígo* yellow spots.

Dothídea ul'mi (Pl. VIII. fig. 24) forms black, slightly raised, and somewhat star-shaped spots upon the upper surface of the leaves of the elm. In a section (fig. 26) the cavities are seen, containing the very delicate asci (fig. 25). The spores (fig. 27) are oval, with a minute septum at one end.

Sphæ'ria rubel'la (Pl. VIII. fig. 16) is extremely common on the dead stems of the nettle, &c. In this Fungus the black bottle-like perithecia (fig. 18), containing the asci and paraphyses (fig. 17), are at first situated beneath the epidermis, through which they at length burst. The spores (fig. 19 *a*) are spindle-shaped, and from four- to seven-septate. When ripe, they escape by a hole or pore in the neck.

Sphæ'ria complanáta (Pl. VIII. fig. 22) is another common species, found in hedges, on dead sticks of the softer (herbaceous) plants, as the parsley-order (Umbelliferæ). Here the minute capsules, which are scattered over the stems, are at first rounded, then flattened on the top (depressed), the neck being very minute (fig. 23). The spores in this species are exceedingly minute, oblong, and not contained in asci.

Sphæ'ria bulláta also belongs to this family. It occurs upon decaying birch-sticks, presenting to the naked eye the appearance represented in Pl. VIII. fig. 20. The black, raised tubercles (receptacles) in their growth burst through the bark, splitting the epidermis. They consist of a white stroma (fig. 20 *a*), in which the bottle-shaped capsules (perithecia) are immersed, the necks projecting slightly above the surface as little points (papillæ). The tufted spore-sacs or asci (fig. 21), with the thread-like paraphyses, are contained within the capsules; and within the asci are the densely packed, very numerous and minute curved spores.

Another species, *Sphæria discifor'mis*, is also common on birch-sticks. It differs from the last in the tubercles being perfectly flat; the spores are also longer, straight, and spindle-shaped (fusiform).

PERISPORÁCEI.—*Erys'iphe guttáta* (Pl.VIII.fig.33) is a member of this family. It appears on the under side of the leaves of the common hazel as a pale spot; and on closely examining it with the naked eye, little black dots are seen scattered on the surface. These are the capsules (conceptacles), which are seated upon straight white filaments. The filaments (*fulcra*) are six or seven in number, and are placed under the capsule, like the legs of a stool (fig. 34); they are rigid, and swollen or inflated at the base (fig. 35). The asci are broad and short, and contain only two spores.

Erysiphe maculáris is the very destructive hop-mildew; and other species are common on various plants.

Chætómium elátum (Pl. VIII. fig. 29) resembles little tufts of brown hairs, occurring upon decaying herbaceous stems. The capsule (fig. 28) is crustaceous, and covered with interlaced, rough, branched hairs (fig. 28 *b*). The spores (fig. 28 *a*) are oval, with a little point at one end (apiculate).

PHYSOMYCÉTES (φῦσα, bladder, μύκης, fungus).— The Fungi belonging to this order include some of the commonest moulds growing upon decaying vegetable substances; while others are found upon leaves, &c. The flocci are generally very evident; and the spores are contained in little naked, bladder-like capsules (*peridíola*) at the ends of free filaments.

MUCORINI.—In this family we have the common mould of paste, *Múcor mucédo* (Pl. VIII. fig. 36). It is easily recognized by the little spherical capsules terminating the long and tufted fruit-stalks (pedicels), which are perceptible to the naked eye. Each capsule consists of a simple enlarged cell, the cavity of which is separated from that of the stalk by a septum. They are white at first, subsequently becoming brown and black. The minute crowded spores (fig. 36 *s*) are at first oblong, afterwards spherical. In the centre of the capsule is a club-shaped body, or *columella* (fig. 36 *a*), formed by the elevation and inflation of the septum.

A beautiful little Fungus of this family, apparently referable to the genus *Acrostalag'mus* (Pl. VIII. fig. 37), is sometimes found upon soft decaying stems. The main filaments are soft, smooth, and not septate. The pedicels are very brittle, whorled, dichotomously branched, scabrous, and terminated each by a little scabrous spherical vesicle (fig. 37 *a*), containing two or three oblong spores.

ANTENNARIÉI.—In this family is *Racódium* (or *Antennária*) *celláre*, the Wine-cellar Fungus, forming the well-known cobweb-like masses hanging from the walls, &c. The little black capsules are seated upon slender septate filaments, and contain numerous round spores.

In examining leaves with the view of procuring Fungi, the reader will most likely meet with the two kinds of bodies represented in Plate VIII. figs. 38 & 39. These are not Fungi, but galls. They arise from an abnormal growth of the leaf-structures, produced by the deposition of the eggs of insects (*Cynipidæ*). The well-known oak-apple, and the red hairy-looking body found upon hedge-roses, are both galls produced in the same way.

Examination and Preservation.—The examination of the Fungi scarcely requires any special remarks.

They should be viewed first as opake objects under a low power; and then sections should be made, or the textures separated with the mounted needles.

There is some difficulty in moistening the smaller filamentous Fungi with water, which is requisite in the determination of the arrangement of the spores upon the branches. Hence the best plan is to lay the Fungus upon a slide, apply a cover, then to add a drop of spirit of wine and afterwards a little water to the edge of the cover. When thus wetted, the spores may be more or less removed with a wet hair-pencil, when the ends of the branches will become perfectly distinct. In examination of the dried smaller Fungi as the *Sphæriæ*, the capsules should be macerated for a time in water.

The softer Fungi are very difficult of preservation in the entire state; but the sections or minute structures may be mounted in chloride of calcium or glycerine.

The harder and drier Fungi may be preserved by drying and gentle pressure between coarse absorbent paper. They may then be glued to pieces of paper and labelled, in the same manner as the flowering plants. Specimens of the capsules, as of the *Sphæriæ*, &c., may also be mounted in the dry state, the asci being preserved in the chloride of calcium or glycerine, in which liquids most of the smaller Fungi will keep extremely well.

PLATE IX.   [PAGE 113.]

ANIMAL TISSUES, &c.

Fig.

Blood-corpuscles, Human.

Blood-corpuscles of Bird (Fowl).

Blood-corpuscles of Reptile(Frog).

Blood-corpuscles of Fish (Stickle-back).

Hair of Bat.

Hair of Mouse.

Hair of Mouse.

Hair, human.

Hair, human.

Wool, fibre of.

Flax, fibres of.

Cotton, fibres of.

Silk, fibres of.

Feather, portion of: *a*, barbs: *b, c*, pinnæ.

Bone, section of: *a*, lacunæ.

Cartilage, section of.

Feather, downy.

Feather, downy: pinna.

Shell, pearly or nacreous portion of.

Muscle: *a*, cellular tissue; *b*, fibrillæ; *c*, bundle of fibrillæ.

Tongue of Whelk: *a*, natural size.

Scale of Dace.

23. Scale of Perch.

24. Scale of Cod.

25. Spermatozoa of Chub.

26. *Flustra foliacea: a*, cells of; *b*, animal, with the tentacles expanded.

27. *Flustra foliacea.*

28. Shell of Oyster, brown portion of.

29. Shell of Oyster, prisms of.

30. *Cyclops quadricornis.*

31. *Daphnia pulex,* female.

32. *Daphnia pulex,* head of male.

33. *Canthocamptus minutus,* an Entomostracan.

34. *Cypris tristriata.*

35. *Cypris tristriata,* eggs of; 35 *a, b, c,* the same hatching.

36. *Acarus domesticus* (Cheese-mite), female.

36*. Cilia of gills of Oyster.

37. *Trombidium fuliginosum: a,* pulp: *b,* mandible; *c,* foot; *d,* natural size; *e,* hair; *f,* hair of *T. holosericeum.*

38. *Acarus domesticus,* male.

39. *Membranipora pilosa.*

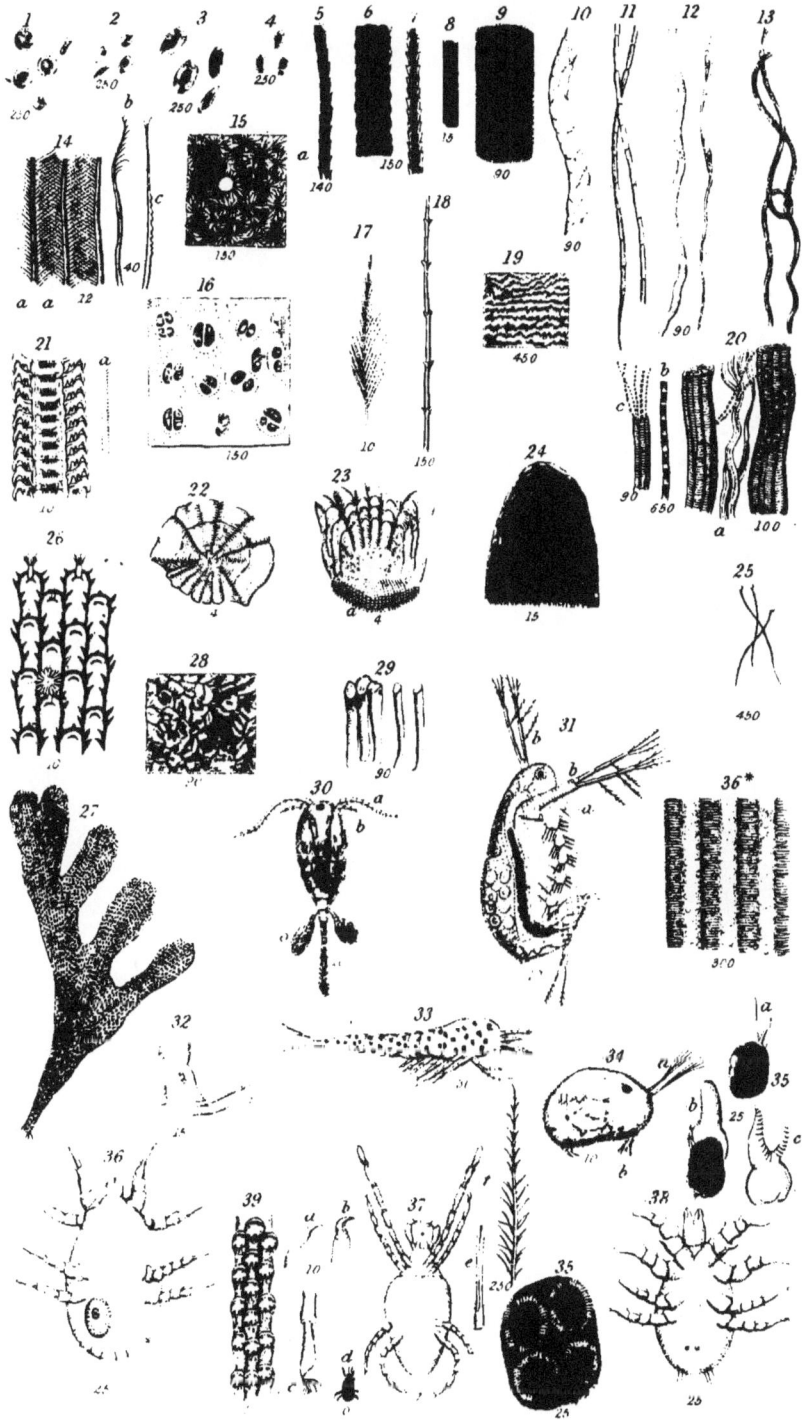

CHAPTER X.

ANIMAL ELEMENTS AND TISSUES.

THE tissues of which animals consist, like those of plants, are primarily derived from cells; in fact the essential part of the egg or óvum, from which all perfect animals originate consists at first only of a simple cell, with its nucleus and nucleolus.

The animal cell-wall differs from that of the vegetable cell in its softness and delicacy—also in its chemical composition,—the former consisting of albúminous (*albúmen*, white of egg) matter, while the latter is composed of cellular or vegetable-cell substance.

There is also a striking difference between vegetable and animal tissues, in the circumstance that, while the former retain their cellular condition to a very great extent, the cells of the latter are frequently so altered by compression and fusion together, or are obscured by the great development of the cell-contents, that the cell-form is obliterated, or can only be discovered by the application of chemical reagents; and in many instances, the relation of the tissues to the cell can only be discovered by tracing the growth or development of the latter from its earliest stages. Hence the examination of the elements and tissues of animals is not well adapted for those who are unpractised in the use of the microscope; and in treating of them, we shall simply notice a few which are most easily examined, beginning with those found in animals belonging to the subkingdom Vertebráta (*ver'tebra*, a spine-bone).

MAMMÁLIA.—The animals belonging to this class

suckle their young; and their blood-vessels contain red blood.

Blood.—This blood consists of a yellowish liquid, in which very numerous red *blood-corpuscles* or globules (Pl. IX. fig. 1) are suspended, and to which the red colour is owing. The blood-corpuscles are not globular, but discoidal, *i. e.* they are circular and flattened, the sides being slightly sunk in. Their form is best seen as they roll over on a slide, after the application of a glass cover. The coloured corpuscles are cells; they appear yellowish red under the microscope, the deep red colour of the blood depending upon the large number of them seen at once and crowded together. It need scarcely be stated that a drop of blood may easily be obtained, by puncturing the wrist with a clean needle. The blood is contained in the blood-vessels. These consist of the ar'teries, which convey the blood from the heart; the veins, which return it to the heart; and a very fine set of intermediate vessels, called the cap'illaries. If a little water be added to a drop of blood on a slide, *colourless corpuscles*, rather larger than the coloured disks, will be seen scattered among the latter. These are the colourless or lymph-corpuscles of the blood. They are truly spherical, and granular on the surface.

Bone.—In examining a transverse section of a bone, one or several very large cavities will be seen with the naked eye in the centre of the section; these contain the marrow, or medulla. In the long bones, the medullary cavity is single, and runs longitudinally down the bone; whilst in the flat bones the cavities are numerous, forming cancelli. Under the microscope, thin transverse sections of bone exhibit oval or rounded holes, or foramina (Pl. IX. fig. 15), which are sections of canals conveying blood-vessels through the bone; these are the *Haver'sian canals.* Around the sections of these canals are seen numerous concentric rings, indicating layers or lamellæ of bony matter.

The substance of bone presents numerous black, somewhat elongated bodies (fig. 15 *a*), called the *lacúnæ*
(*lacúna*, a little hollow) or bone-corpuscles, which are
however hollow, therefore not truly corpuscles, as
they were formerly considered. Between the adjacent
lacunæ run numerous fine, dark, branched lines, consisting of very minute canals, or *canalic'uli*. If the
section of bone be viewed by reflected light, the
lacunæ and canaliculi will appear white. In the dried
bone they contain air.

The structure of bone is best seen when viewed as
a transparent object in the dry state; for when the
section is immersed in liquid, the lacunæ and canaliculi become filled up.

The size and form of the bone-corpuscles and canaliculi vary in different animals, so much so that the
Class or Order to which an animal belongs may be
determined by reference to these particulars.

Bone consists of earthy salts deposited in a finely
granular form throughout the substance of cartilage.
By soaking a piece of bone in vinegar or other dilute
acid, the earthy salts will be dissolved, the soft cartilage being left. But the structure of cartilage may be
best observed by making thin sections of the gristle
covering the ends of bones. It exhibits a bluish-
white basis (Pl. IX. fig. 16), in which are imbedded
numerous cells or *cartilage-corpuscles*, often undergoing cell-division. In some kinds of cartilage, the
basis is composed of fibres.

Muscle.—On examining a piece of the red flesh of
an animal under a low power, the mass will exhibit
a number of coarse, parallel, longitudinal, dark lines
(Pl. IX. fig. 20), the substance between these lines
being marked with cross or transverse striæ, or lines,
and with fine longitudinal lines. The coarse longitudinal lines indicate the intervals between bundles of
slender fibres, or *fibril'læ*, of which muscle consists.
The fibrillæ (fig. 20 *b, c*) are very difficult to separate;

but when perfectly separated, they are seen to be exceedingly slender, and to consist of alternately light and dark portions in regular series. When the fibrillæ of the bundles are in close apposition, as in the natural muscle, the dark portions, being in the same lines, by their coincidence form the transverse striæ. The bundles into which they are combined are surrounded by a delicate skin or membrane, with a little cellular tissue.

The structure of muscle may be observed in a piece of ham which has been soaked for a day or two in spirit of wine, the mounted needles being used to pick it to pieces.

The above-mentioned transversely striated muscular fibre is that found in the voluntary muscles, or those under the influence of the will. But there are other muscles in animals which are involuntary, or not subject to the will; in these the fibrillar structure is absent, the muscular tissue consisting of simple elongated and nucleated cells.

Cel'lular tissue—This fills the interstices between the other tissues and organs of animals, in the same manner that the vegetable parenchyma does those of plants. It is not, however, composed of cells, but of very fine, soft, colourless, and wavy fibres (Pl. VIII. fig. 20 *a*), aggregated into bundles, which interlace so as to leave spaces or aréolæ between them.

The cellular or areolar tissue may be found in a piece of beef or mutton, in the intervals of the muscular fibres.

Skin.—The skin is composed of cellular tissue, its outer surface presenting a number of projecting blunt points, called *papil'læ*. It contains a large number of blood-vessels; and when the capillaries are well filled by injection with a coloured composition, it forms a beautiful microscopic object.

The skin is covered by the epider'mis or cuticle,

which consists of several layers of cells. It is the epidermis which is raised and covers the bladders formed by the action of a blister applied to the skin.

Hair.—The hair consists of long solid filaments (Pl. IX. fig. 9), and not of hollow tubes, as was formerly supposed. It presents varieties of structure in different animals, which agree generally in animals belonging to the same Orders.

Hairs are implanted in pits in the skin; each is swollen at the base to form the bulb, which is seated upon a papilla of the skin, by which it is formed or secreted. The hair is an epidermic formation, consisting of epidermic cells more or less flattened and altered in shape by mutual pressure.

The colour of the hair is usually seated in the outer or cortical portion of the stem or shaft, and arises from the presence of aggregations of minute granules of colouring-matter or *pigment*, as the colouring-matter of animals is called : in the human hair it forms short longitudinal stripes (fig. 9). In the central pith or medullary portion of the hair the cellular structure is more open and distinct than in the cortical portion, in which the cells are so compressed and consolidated as only to exhibit the cell-structure after treatment with reagents; and the medullary cells often contain air.

In grey or white hairs, the whiteness depends mainly upon the presence of air in the cells of the pith. In the gnawing or rodent animals, as the mouse or the rabbit, the pigment is partially at least situated in the cells of the medulla.

In the hairs of many animals, the cuticular or surface-cells of the shaft are distinctly imbricated (fig. 5), and form beautiful microscopic objects.

The principal interest in the structure of the hair relates to the three points above mentioned, viz. the position of the pigment, the arrangement of the cuticular cells or scales, and that of the cells of the pith.

The pigment is best examined in hairs moistened with a little spirit of wine, which displaces the air from the cells of the pith, and renders the hair transparent; a little water should be subsequently added. The cuticular scales are also well shown by this proceeding. Towards the root of the hairs in the mouse, they project beyond the margin, giving it a toothed or dentate appearance; in the hair of the mole, the bat (fig. 5), or the wolf, this dentation may also be seen. In the hairs of some of the foreign bats, the scales are whorled, forming very beautiful objects.

The cells of the pith (Pl. IX. fig. 7) also present interesting varieties, being sometimes arranged in a single row, at others in two or more rows (fig. 6). These are best seen in hairs recently immersed in spirit or in oil of turpentine; for if the hair be too long soaked in these liquids, the air will be entirely displaced by them. The cells of the pith appear black by transmitted and white by reflected light, in the dry hairs, from the presence of air. They may be well examined in the hair of the mouse (figs. 6 & 7), or in that of the mole. Wool, which is the hair of the sheep, consists of curled fibres (Pl. IX. fig. 10), in which the imbricated arrangement of the surface-scales is very distinctly seen.

In Pl. IX. figs. 10–13 the fibres of wool, flax or woody fibre, cotton, and silk are represented together, to allow of comparison; for the microscope is of great assistance in discriminating these substances when existing in textile fabrics. The fibres of wool (fig. 10) are distinguished by their solidity, wavyness, and the imbricated scales; those of flax (fig. 11) by their thick walls, great length, acute ends, and their knotty appearance at intervals. The fibres of cotton (fig. 12) are soft, flaccid, flattened, and often twisted; and those of silk (fig. 13) are solid and very slender. By a little chemical testing, the discrimination is made still more easy; but for an account of this I must refer to the Dictionary.

BIRDS.—In the Class of Birds, the structure of the *feathers* deserves special notice. Feathers are epidermic formations, or consist of aggregations of epidermic cells, yet so altered by compression and fusion together that the cell-structure is in most parts difficult to detect. In a feather three parts are distinguishable,—the transparent cylindrical quill; its opake continuation, which is more or less flattened at the sides, forming the shaft; and the vanes or beards, which arise from the sides of the shaft, consisting of numerous closely set, parallel, flattened fibres, called the barbs. The structure of the barbs forms the interesting object to the microscopist. On examining a piece of the coloured vane of a somewhat large feather (Pl. IX. fig. 14), a row of fine parallel colourless filaments (*pinnæ*) will be observed, arising from the opposite sides, the filaments of one side lying obliquely across those arising from the other; and while the filaments or pinnæ of one side present a row of little teeth (fig. 14 *c*) near their base, those of the opposite side (fig. 14 *b*) are provided with as many hooks near their apex, which curve over the teeth to connect the barbs together. This curious arrangement is adapted to keep the parts of the feather firmly united, and yet to allow of their play and flexibility. To observe this structure, a portion of a vane should be soaked in oil of turpentine, and mounted in balsam.

In the downy feathers (Pl. IX. fig. 17) the barbs are not furnished with the pinnæ, but present simply whorls of minute spines (fig. 18).

The *bones* of birds present the same general structure as that of mammals, the lacunæ being, however, more numerous and smaller.

The *blood* of birds (Pl. IX. fig. 2) differs entirely from that of mammals, in the red corpuscles being oval instead of circular, and convex instead of concave; and each contains a distinct oval and granular nucleus.

REPTILES.—In reptiles, as the frog, toad, or water-lizard (*Triton*), the bone-corpuscles or lacunæ are larger and more numerous than in either of the former classes; and the blood-corpuscles (Pl. IX. fig. 3) are comparatively very large, oval, rather concave, and contain a large granular nucleus.

The smooth water-newt or triton, properly called *Lissotriton punctátus*, is a very interesting animal in a microscopic point of view.   It may be found in most ponds; and if several are removed in a net, and kept in a large glass jar, with water-plants, they will live for a long period.   In the spring or early summer they will deposit their eggs upon the aquatic plants, generally on the under surface of a leaf, which they bend downwards, so as to protect them.   The eggs or ova, are about half the size of a pea, and consist of a sac containing a transparent liquid, with a yellowish globule within.   After a time these eggs will hatch, and the larvæ or young newts must be removed from the water, otherwise the parents will devour them.

If one of these larvæ, which resemble little fish in appearance, be placed with a little water in the "live-box," and the cap be very gently pressed down, so as to fix the body of the animal, the circulation of the blood may be very beautifully seen in either the fringe-like gills, which are placed on each side of the neck, or in the tail, a low power being used; at the same time the beautiful stellate pigment-cells of the skin will be observed.   The structure of the rudimentary spinal column, which runs down the middle of the back, and consists of simple large cartilage-cells, may also be made out, when the animal is dead, by a little dissection with the aid of needles.

FISHES.—In the fourth class of vertebrate animals,

which consists of the fishes, we find interesting structures in the blood, the scales, and the roe. The corpuscles of the blood (Pl. IX. fig. 4) differ from those of the
Mammalia, but agree with those of birds and reptiles,
in being oval instead of round. The scales of fishes
(Pl. IX. figs. 22, 23) are usually rounded or oval,
as in most of our freshwater fishes, when they are
called cyc'loid (κύκλος, circle) ; but sometimes they
are toothed at one end (fig. 23 a), forming cténoid
(κτείς, a comb) scales, as in the perch. Most scales
exhibit a number of concentric rings, which are the
indications of laminæ; and many of them are lobed
at the margin, sometimes also having radiate furrows.
In the centre are often seen little rounded solid
bodies, having somewhat the appearance of cells,
which are very well seen in the scales of the perch ;
and in some scales these bodies are arranged in
concentric rows throughout the substance, as in
those of the eel or the cod (fig. 24). The substance
of which scales consist is generally cartilaginous; in
some of them, however, true bony matter is present.
Fish-scales are contained within the substance of the
skin, and not merely attached to it by one end, as
appears to be the case in many fishes. In most of
our common fishes, as the roach or perch, the scales
project beyond the level of the skin ; but the projecting
portion is covered by a thin layer of the skin; and
when the scales are scraped off, this layer, with its
elegant stellate pigment-cells, is usually found adherent to it. In some other fishes, as the cod and
eel, the scales are entirely sunk below the surface;
and these are commonly supposed to have no scales.
They may, however, be easily found by dissection,
or by drying a piece of the skin under pressure between two plates of glass, and mounting a portion
in balsam.

The beautiful silvery lustre of the skin of fishes
depends upon the presence of innumerable very minute

M

and thin crystals ; these may be well examined in the skin of a sprat.

The roe of fishes consists of the ova or eggs, and the spermatozoa,—the ova being contained in the hard, the spermatozoa in the soft roe. The eggs consist of a cell surrounded by one or two membranes; and the latter are often traversed by numerous fine radial canals, or present a funnel-shaped tube leading to the ovum. The spermatozoa of the soft roe consist of exceedingly slender filaments (fig. 25), terminated at one end by a kind of head. The reader will not fail to detect the analogy between the ovum of the animal and that of the ovule of the plant ; and it need scarcely be stated that the spermatozoa of the animal fertilize the ova, in the same manner that the pollen-tubes and spermatozoa of plants fertilize the ovules existing in them. In the case of fishes, the spermatozoa of the soft roe escaping into the water, and moved by the ciliary action of the filament, enter the micropyle-like canals of the ova, which are deposited by the fish upon the bottom of rivers.

The scales of fishes may be prepared for examination by scraping them off and macerating them in water until the adherent portion of the skin is softened and decomposed, so that it may be washed away. They should be dried between glass plates, and viewed under a low power, as dry transparent objects.

The structure of muscle can be more easily made out in fishes than in other animals. A portion of the flesh should be macerated in spirit as directed above.

Mollus'ca.—We shall now leave the vertebrate animals, and pass to the subkingdom Mollusca, the marine kinds of which are popularly called shell-fish : three of their structures form interesting objects for examination—the shell, the tongue, and the gills.

Shell.—The general structure of the shell of the

Mollusca may be illustrated by reference to that of the oyster. Two kinds of shell-substance are at once distinguishable in an oyster-shell, an outer brown, and an inner pearly or nacreous. The brown portion exhibits under the microscope the appearance of a cell-structure (Pl. IX. fig. 28), the angular forms from mutual pressure being very distinct. The component bodies of this portion are seen to be more or less elongated and flattened in the side view, forming prisms (fig. 29). The structure of the pearly part of the shell is more difficult of examination, and can only be seen distinctly in ground and polished sections. In these, under a high power, it exhibits numerous fine, somewhat parallel wavy lines (fig. 19), which are the indications of thin layers, or laminæ, of which it is composed.

Shell consists of a basis of animal matter in which carbonate of lime (chalk) is deposited, the whole being poured out or secreted by the skin or mantle of the mollusk.

Pearls, which possess the same structure as the nacreous part of shell, consist of the nacre formed around some foreign body, as a grain of sand, &c., by which the mantle has been wounded.

Tongue.—The structure of the tongue of the Mollusca is very interesting, on account of the curious teeth which are found upon it. It may be illustrated by the common Whelk (*Buc'cinum unda'tum*), which is sold at the street-stalls. As, to one unacquainted with the anatomy of the Mollusca, there is some difficulty in finding the tongue, it may be well to point out how it is to be found. If the shell containing the animal be placed so that its orifice is directed upwards, the point or apex of the spire being towards the reader, the lid (oper'culum) which closes the shell will be at once evident. On drawing the animal from the shell by means of the lid, the foot or portion which is applied by the animal to the surface upon

which it creeps will be seen. At the upper part of
this is the head, with its two horns (ten'tacles).
Below the roots or bases of the tentacles, and between them and the upper part of the foot, is
the little round mouth. On slitting this up with
scissors, a cavity will be opened, and in it will be
seen a reddish tube (the proboscis), about as large as
a goose-quill, with an aperture at the end. This
must be carefully slit up, when the tongue, which is
of about the size of a crow-quill, will come into view.
The tongue is moveable in the proboscis, and can be
protruded or withdrawn by the animal at will. If
the surface of the tongue be viewed under a hand-
lens, the rows of teeth will be seen at once. It is
better not to pull the tongue out with forceps, as
the teeth are easily displaced and injured. The best
plan is to dissect away the muscular structures with
forceps and a pair of fine-pointed scissors, then to
cut off the tongue at its root, and to soak it in water
for some hours, when the skin or epidermis containing
the teeth can be separated with the mounted needles
under a simple lens or microscope. After any loose
particles have been washed away with a hair pencil,
the object may be spread flat on a slide, and dried
between two slides. The upper slide should then be
removed, the tongue soaked in oil of turpentine, and
mounted in balsam with the least possible heat.

As thus prepared, the horny teeth (Pl. IX. fig. 21)
are seen to be arranged in rows, united by a colourless
membrane, so as to form a long ribbon. The teeth
form three longitudinal parallel rows, a central and
two lateral. Each tooth, considering the separate
pieces as constituting distinct teeth, has little teeth
or denticles at its lower edge. These are curved
inwards, four in number, and connected by a basal
plate in the side teeth; while the middle teeth have
six or seven straight denticles. These teeth serve
to enable the animal to scrape or rasp the algæ,

and other matters forming their food, from the surfaces upon which they grow. And if some water-snails are placed in a glass jar the inside of which is covered with confervoid growths, the curious patterns left after the action of the snails' tongues will be found to present a very curious appearance.

Gills.—The gills or "beards" of the oyster or mussel exhibit very strikingly the phenomenon of ciliary motion. The gills (branchiæ) are respiratory organs, consisting of folds of the skin, covered with cilia, by means of which the water in which the animal lives is set in motion, and constantly changed to aërate the blood within them. The currents thus induced serve also to bring the food which floats in the water towards the mouth of the animal. By snipping off a thin portion of one of the brown beards of a fresh oyster, laying it upon a slide, adding a drop of the "liquor" contained within the shell, and lightly pressing a cover upon the whole, the remarkable phenomenon to one who has not before viewed it will be seen under a somewhat high power—about $\frac{1}{4}$-inch. The whole field will appear in motion, and the lashing or whip-like action of the cilia will be seen, especially towards the edges of the bars (Pl. IX. fig. 36) of the gills. The rapid motion of any floating particles present will also be noticed, showing the direction of the currents of liquid, which, as the liquid is transparent, would not otherwise be recognizable.

BRYOZÓA (βρύον, moss, ζῶον, animal).—The animals included in this Class, which belongs to the Mollusca, are mostly marine. They are microscopic, and contained in horny or calcareous sacs or cells, aggregated together to form polyp'idoms (*pol'ype*, and δῶμα, a house). They are sometimes plant-like or leafy (Pl. IX. fig. 27), at others filamentous and branched, or they form a layer or crust upon the objects to which they are attached. The polypidoms, which are often some inches in length, are frequently met with on the sea-shore, the cells (fig. 26 *a*) having slit-like valvular orifices. The bodies of the animals are soft and polype-like, and are furnished at one end with a circle of tentacles, covered with rows of cilia, by which the water is changed for respiration, and particles of food are brought to the mouth. The tentacles can be protruded or withdrawn at the will of the animal. The Bryozoa are what are called compound animals, each individual body having its own set of organs; yet the whole are connected together.

The two species figured are very common. *Flus'tra foliácea* (Pl. IX. fig. 27) is found everywhere upon the sea-shore. The polypidom has cells upon both sides; and they are narrowed at one end, and rounded at the other. *Membranip'ora pilósa* (Pl. IX. fig. 39) occurs upon sea-weeds and other marine bodies, forming a closely adherent layer. The orifices of the cells are surrounded with teeth, and are usually furnished below with a very long bristle—the polypidom appearing to the naked eye as a white hairy crust. In the variety figured, the long bristles are replaced by a spine; and this is not uncommon.

The polypidoms of the Bryozoa form interesting microscopic objects, the cells being furnished with variously arranged spines and punctures or dots. In some the cells are erect and arranged in rows upon the branches of a plant-like stem, while in others they are scattered irregularly over a creeping filament.

For examination they should be prepared by maceration in fresh water, and drying between glass plates or sheets of paper, and either viewed as opake objects or, after soaking in turpentine and mounting in balsam, as transparent objects.

It may be remarked that the name Bryozoa for this class of Mollusca, which was thoroughly established, has recently been changed in this country to Polyzóa (πολὺς, many, ζῶον, animal), and that the name of polypidom has been altered to polyzóary.

CHAPTER XI.

ARTICULATA (ARTIC'ULUS, A JOINT).

THE animals belonging to this subkingdom are specially distinguished by the body and limbs being jointed: as familiar instances, may be mentioned the lobster, the wood-louse, spiders, insects, and worms.

Taking the class Crustacea, to which the two first animals belong, we find interesting microscopic forms in the subclass Entomos'traca (ἔντομον, insect; ὄστρακον, shell).

ENTOMOSTRACA.—The animals contained in this Order are met with in every pool or pond, some of them inhabiting the sea. They are mostly minute, yet visible to the naked eye, forming specks swimming actively or leaping through the water; hence some of them have been called water-fleas. The body of the animal is protected by a shell or car'apace, which in some consists of a single piece (Pl. IX. fig. 30), while in others it consists of two similar parts or valves (fig. 31), in the latter case the joints of the body being indistinctly visible. The head is furnished with usually two projecting feelers or antennæ (*anten'na*, a sail-yard), one of which is uppermost or superior (Pl. IX. figs. 30, 31, 34 *a*), the other lowermost or inferior (figs. 30 and 34 *b*); and these are often used for swimming. The antennæ are jointed, and sometimes beautifully plúmose (*pluma*, a feather) or feathery, *i. e.* furnished with rows of long and very slender filaments. There are several pairs of jointed legs, some of which serve as jaws (foot-jaws), while others are finely filamentous to serve for swimming and as respiratory organs (branchial feet). The four species figured are very common.

Cypris tristriáta (Pl. IX. fig. 34) is found in ponds and ditches. The carapace is bivalve, or has two valves, which are convex and oval; and it is of a greenish colour, with three irregular dark stripes behind. The superior antennæ (*a*) are jointed and finely feathery, the inferior antennæ (*b*) having a tuft or pencil of fine filaments arising from their anterior margin. The eye is single. The animal swims steadily and freely through the water.

The eggs of *Cypris* (Pl. IX. fig. 35) are often found in glasses of water containing the animals. They are rounded or oblong, of a red colour, glued together by an amorphous jelly, and adherent to pieces of stick or the sides of the glass. They are enclosed in a thick shell, which exhibits a cellular appearance in the surface view, and is striated in the side view; so that the structure of the shell is prismatic, as in that of the oyster. When the eggs escape from the shell, they present the appearance represented in fig. 35 *a*, the body of the young animal being enclosed in a transparent envelope, one end of which forms a blunt protrusion; there is also a separate slender process enclosing the superior antennæ. After a time, the envelope is cast off (fig. 35 *b*), when the animal begins its active stage of life. The cast-off envelopes (fig. 35 *c*), with the protruded portions wrinkled, are often found in the sediment of water containing the animals. The structure of these ova is that of what are called winter ova, which agree with the resting-spores of the lower plants or the Algæ.

Cy'clops quadricor'nis (Pl. IX. fig. 30) is another common species. In this the body is closely surrounded by the jointed shell, as in a lobster. The superior antennæ (*a*) are very long and many-jointed, each joint having short bristles arising from it, while the inferior antennæ are short and four-jointed. There is no separate head, this being united to or consolidated with the first joint of the thor'ax or chest, the head and thorax together comprising four joints. The remaining joints enclose the belly, or abdómen, which has the appearance of a tail; but the tail is constituted by the two last parallel pieces, which are furnished with fine feathery filaments.

The female is most commonly met with, and is easily known by having the egg-pouch, or ovary (o) external on each side, and filled with eggs or ova. The little *Cyclops* is readily recognized by its form and jerking motion through the water.

Daph'nia púlex (Pl. IX. fig. 31) is a very common Entomostracan, and is very well adapted to illustrate the structure, on account of its size and transparence. In this animal the body is loosely connected with a bivalve shell, which, on careful examination, is seen to be reticulated or marked with net-like lines. The superior antennæ (a) are very small, placed under a small beak, and have at the end a minute tuft of hairs. The inferior antennæ (b) resemble arms, being large and branched; and by means of them the animal rows itself through the water. The structure of the eye is curious, consisting of a number of round lenses aggregated together, the fine muscular threads by which it is moved being easily distinguished with a high power. The legs are flattened, and furnished with elegant feathery sétæ (*seta*, a bristle), serving as gills or branchiæ. They are constantly in motion, fanning the water so as to change incessantly the portion with which they are in contact. About the middle of the back is placed the little transparent heart, with its colourless blood, which may be distinctly seen beating, or contracting and dilating, in the living animal; and between the back of the animal and the shell are seen the ova, which remain there until they are hatched.

The genera and species of the Entomostraca are very numerous. Those mentioned above will serve

to illustrate the general structure of the order.   To
distinguish the man′dibles (*mandib′ula,* a jaw) or
proper jaws, the foot-jaws, and the branchial legs,
the animals must be dissected in water with the
mounted needles.   The very delicate feathery filaments of the branchiæ may be best observed when
these organs are dried on a slide.

The Entromostaca may be kept alive in a jar
of water with water-plants for a long period.   They
may be removed from the water for examination
by the dipping-tube, and are best · observed in a live-
box.

ARACH′NIDA (ἀράχνη, spider) is the Class of spiders,
scorpions, and mites.

Aranéida.—This Order contains the more highly
developed forms of the Class, among which are the
common spiders of houses and gardens ; and some of
their structures are very curious and interesting.

The head of spiders is united or fused with the
thorax, forming one piece, which is called the *ceph′alo-
thorax* (κεφαλή, head, θώραξ, chest).

The claw-jaws, or *man′dibles,* are terminated by a
curved and pointed claw, with which the spiders hold
their prey.   It is traversed by a slender canal, containing a slender tube or duct leading from a poison-
gland, and opening near its point ; and when the
insect prey is transfixed by the mandible, the poison
is pressed out and enters the wound.

Near the root or base of the mandibles on each
side is a jointed feeler, or pal′pus ; but spiders have
no anten′næ.   The eyes are simple, forming separate
round shining dots, and are called *ocel′li* (*ocel′lus,*
a little eye) ; they are usually placed on the top of
the head, and are often arranged in a geometrical
form, as a triangle, &c.

The legs are four pairs ; they are hairy, and terminated by two or three claws, which are fringed
with minute teeth, or pec′tinate.   These claws serve

to comb the fibres of the web, just as we comb our hair with a common comb.

The *spinnerets*, with which spiders form their web, are very curious organs. They are situated at the under and hind part of the body, and consist of two or three cones, or papillæ, on each side. On the summits of these papillæ are very numerous bristle-like tubes, through which the secretion of certain glands passes; this secretion, when hardened by exposure to the air, forms the fibres of the web.

On carefully examining a spider's web, the radial fibres, or those which pass from the centre to the circumference, will be found to be smooth, these fibres serve to fix the web; while the cross fibres are covered with numerous viscid globules, which serve to attach flies or other prey to them. This difference of the fibres is best observed with a hand-lens.

ACARÍNA, or the Order of Mites.—Here belongs cheese-mite, *Ac'arus domes'ticus* (Pl. IX. fig. 36). Its body is somewhat milky white, oval, and furnished with feathery hairs. When viewed from beneath, there is seen a transverse line, indicating the separation of the thorax from the abdomen; and another line in front of this, with four minute tubercles, from each of which arises a hair. The head is pointed and beak-like, forming a *ros'trum* (*rostrum*, a beak), consisting of two mandibles pressed together; these can only be seen to be separate when dissected apart with the mounted needles. Each mandible is chélate (χηλὴ, forceps), or has the form of a lobster's claw; and beneath the two mandibles is a flat membranous under lip or labium, consolidated on each side with a palp. The legs are four pairs, as in all the Arachnida; they are pinkish, 6-jointed, and terminated by a leaf-like sucker and a minute claw.

The males (fig. 38) are smaller than the females, the fore legs being much stouter, and furnished with a blunt tooth (fig. 38 *a*). The eggs can often be dis-

tinguished within the body of the female (fig. 36);
they are oval and granular.

Another species of *Acarus*, *A. sac'chari*, is found
abundantly in ordinary moist sugar. If a little of
the sugar be placed in a wine-glass, some water added,
and the mixture be stirred until the sugar is dissolved,
the *Acari* will be found both in the sediment and
floating on the surface.

A somewhat larger member of the order occurs as
a parasite upon a species of Dung-beetle (*Geotrúpes
stercorárius*) which is vulgarly known as the Lousy
Watchman. The beetle is black, shaded with
purple, about three-quarters of an inch long, and is
found under cow-dung. The mites cling pertinaci-
ously to the under parts of the beetle, and can easily
be seen with the naked eye. They are whitish, with
the mandibles, the sucker, and two claws very distinct; and the palpi are unattached to the labium,
or free. These mites form the species *Gam'asus
coleoptrator'um*. Another species, *Gamasus telárius*,
is the red spider of the greenhouse.

Trombid'ium fuliginósum (Pl. IX. fig. 37 *d*) is a
common red spider of gardens. It is of a scarlet
colour, appearing velvety from the presence of a dense
coat of feathery hairs (fig. 37 *f*). The palpi of this
mite are large, free, the last joint but one (Pl. IX.
fig. 37 *a*) being furnished with a claw, while the last
joint is obtuse, and resembles a lateral appendage.
The mandibles (fig. 37 *b*) are furnished with a sharp
curved claw. The legs are long, especially the anterior pair, and terminated by two claws, with a delicate sucker-like appendage (fig. 37 *c*).

Another species of *Trombidium*, *T. holoseric'eum*,
greatly resembling the last, is also found in gardens.
It may be easily distinguished from the last by the
club-shaped hairs (fig. 37 *e*) existing upon the body.
The harvest-bug, which causes such irritation of the
legs of persons who frequent corn-fields in the

PLATE X. [PAGE 133.]

INSECTS.

Fig.
1. *Atropos pulsatorius* : * natural size.
2. *Aphis* of Geranium: *a*, foot; *b*, anal tube; *c*, antenna.
3. Scales on wing of Apollo-butterfly.
4. *Lithobius forcipatus.*
5. *Lithobius forcipatus*, head of: *a*, antennæ; *b*, mandibles; *c*, labial palpi; *d*, labium.
6. *Dytiscus marginalis*, head of larva.
7. Young larva of *Dytiscus marginalis.*
8. Pupa of Gnat (*Culex pipiens*).
9. Larva of Gnat.
10. Head of Gnat, male.
11. Head of Gnat, female.
12. *Coccinella 7-punctata* (large Ladybird), labium of.
13. *Coccinella 7-punctata*, mandible of.
14. *Coccinella 7-punctata*, labrum of.
15. *Coccinella 7-punctata*, antenna of.
16. *Coccinella 7-punctata*, maxilla of: *a*, palp; *b*, *c*, lobes of maxilla.
17. Head of *Musca domestica* (Housefly) : *a*, antenna; *b*, labial palpi; *c*, proboscis.
18. Head of *Stomoxys calcitrans* : 18 *a*, antenna.
19. Scales of insects: *a*, scale of *Podura*; *b*, of House-moth (*Tinea*

Fig.
vestianella); *c*, of *Podura* ; *d*, of *Lepisma*; *e*, hair of *Podura*; *f*, scale of Cabbage-Butterfly (*Pontia brassicæ*).
20. Head of Cabbage-Butterfly: *a*, antennæ broken off; *b*, palp; *c*, tongue (antlia); *d*, club of antenna.
21. Head of human Flea (*Pulex irritans*), female (♀): *a*, palpi; *b*, maxillæ.
22. Flea of the Rat (*Pulex muris*), male (♂).
23. *Pterostichus* (*Steropus*) *madidus*; 23 *a*, antenna.
24. Part of leg of *Pterostichus madidus*: *a*, tibia; *b*, tarsus.
25. Labrum of *Pterostichus madidus.*
26. Mandible of *Pterostichus madidus.*
27. Labium of *Pterostichus madidus* : *a*, mentum; *b*, labial palp.
28. Maxilla of *Pterostichus madidus* : *a*, claw; *b*, *c*, maxillary palps.
29. Proboscis of House-fly.
30. Larva of Flea.
31. Larva of *Chironomus plumosus.*
32. Foot of House-fly.
33. Eye of House-fly.
34. Leg of Ant (*Formica fusca*); 34*, pectinate process.

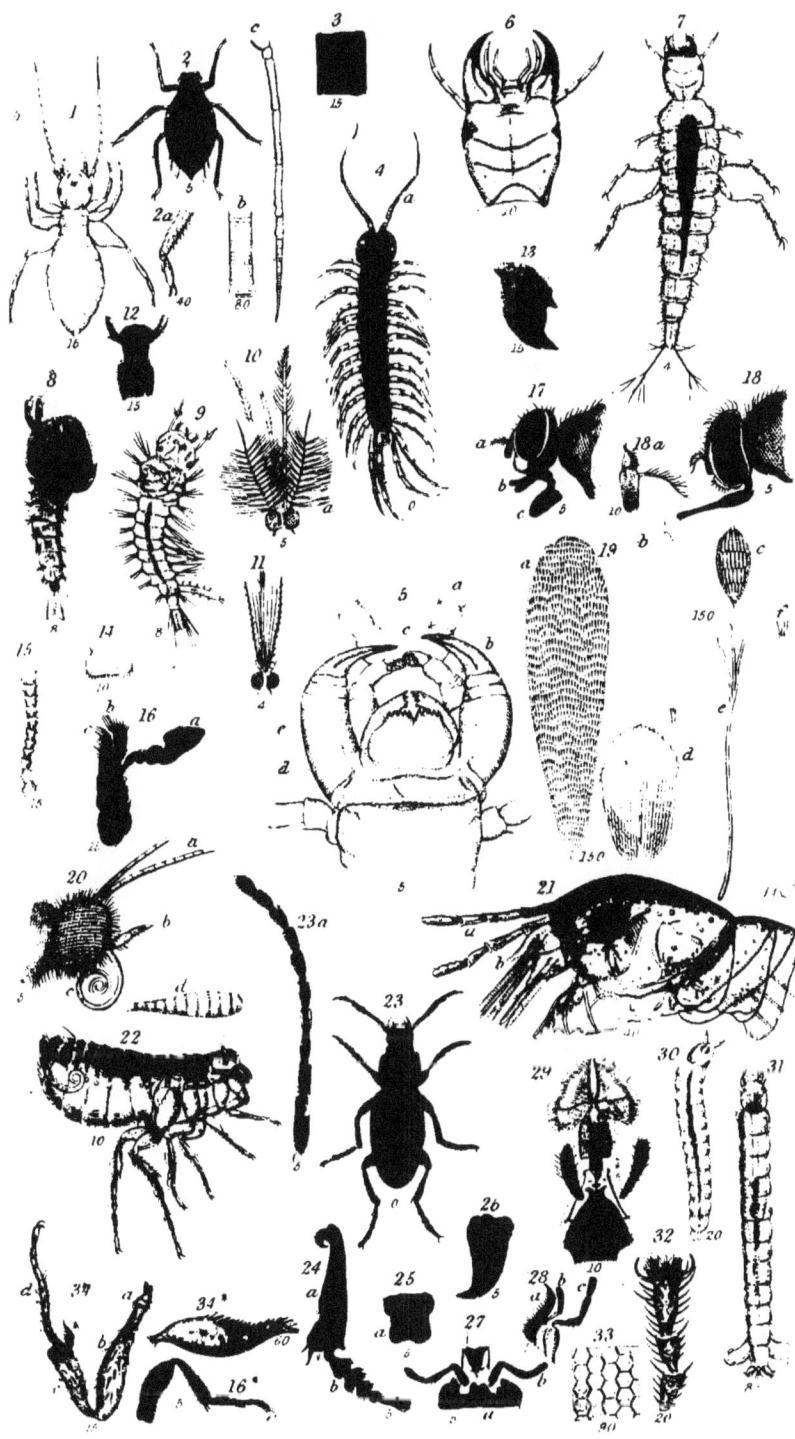

autumn, is also a species of *Trombidium*—*T. autumnále.*

Preparation.—The organs of the mouth, &c., of the Spiders are easily prepared for examination, by carefully pulling them off with forceps or the mounted needles, then drying them under pressure between two glass slips, macerating in turpentine, and mounting in balsam. Those of the Acarina should be dissected out with the needles, after the body has been crushed in a drop of water on a slide, and the internal substance has been gently washed away with a hair pencil. They may then be dried on a slide, with a cover laid on, and turpentine applied to the edge of the cover, balsam being added when most of this has evaporated. The various parts may also be mounted in chloride of calcium or glycerine.

INSECTS.—The members of the class of Insects are extremely interesting to the microscopic observer, not only on account of the beautiful structures which they present, but also from these being comparatively large, usually coloured, and easily distinguished under the lower powers. Hence they form admirable objects for study to those who are but little accustomed to the use of the microscope.

MYRIAP′ODA (μύριος, myriad, πούς, foot.— This Order contains those insects which are popularly known as the hundred-legs and millepedes; by many zoologists they have been arranged in a distinct class.

The most common member of this Order is *Lithóbius forcipátus* (Pl. X. fig. 4), which is found under stones, in cellars, and among garden-rubbish. It is of a yellowish-brown colour, with long, many-jointed, gradually tapering or setáceous (*séta*, a bristle) antennæ (figs. 4 *a*, 5 *a*), and two large and powerful mandibles (fig. 5 *b*) resembling those of the spiders. It has also a broad, notched, and toothed lower lip, or labium (fig. 5 *d*), above which are two toothed jaws,

N

or maxillæ, and two lip-feelers, or labial palpi (*c*). The eyes consist of a group of ocelli on each side (*e*). The body is protected by alternately larger and smaller dorsal plates, which are fifteen in number; and there are fifteen pairs of legs, which are terminated by a single claw.   On the sides of the body will be found some oval dark-looking bodies, fringed with hairs; these are the spir'acles (*spirac'ulum*, a breathing-hole) or breathing-pores.   They form the orifices of certain branched and transversely striated tubes, which are distributed throughout the body; the tubes are called *tráchee* (*trachea*, the windpipe), and their walls contain an elastic spiral fibre which keeps them open. These parts of the insect can only be distinctly seen when the body has been slit up on the under side; and, after washing away the animal matter with water by the aid of a hair pencil, pressed between two slides with a clip, dried, soaked in turpentine, and mounted in balsam.

THYSANÚRA (*θύσανοι*, fringe, *ούρὰ*, tail).—The insects belonging to the genus *Podúra*, of this Order, are very minute and difficult to examine; but they are specially interesting, on account of the structure of their scales.   They are common in gardens and cellars, under flower-pots, &c., and are about one-tenth of an inch long.   They are of a brownish or silvery-leaden colour, wingless, with six legs, and when touched they leap like a flea.   The leaping motion is produced by the action of the tail, which is forked and bent under the body.

The body is usually covered with minute scales (Pl. X. fig. 19, *a, c*), and these are used as test-objects. The structure of the scales varies in the different genera and species; those usually used (fig. 19 *a*) are stated to belong to *Podúra plum'bea*; it appears, however, that this is not correct.   The scales sold as test-objects under this name are covered with minute and short raised lines (fig. 19 *a*), arranged in irregular but somewhat parallel wavy rows. It requires a good microscope and a high power to show them distinctly, and they should appear perfectly black and separate. The little lines are much coarser in some scales than in others; so that there are easy and difficult scales, as they are called.

The *Poduræ* may be caught by holding a sheet of paper near their haunts and disturbing them; and when they have jumped upon the paper, a slide laid upon them and gently pressed will remove some of the scales for examination.

The scales should be mounted as dry transparent objects; for if wetted, they become very transparent, and the markings appear removed, which however is not really the case.

The scales of *Lepis'ma saccharína* (Pl. X. fig. 19 *d*), a member of this Order, were formerly used as test-objects; but they are too easily made out to serve for this purpose with modern microscopes. The insect is not common. The scales (fig. 19 *d*) exhibit continuous nearly parallel longitudinal lines or ribs.

ANOPLÚRA (ἄνοπλος, unarmed, οὐρά, tail).—This third Order of insects consists of the Lice of the Mammalia and birds. They are minute, resembling mites to the naked eye, but may be at once distinguished from them by the distinct head and thorax and the presence of six instead of eight legs.

Some of them are suctorial, *i. e.* have a short and slender tube, with which they suck the blood of the animals of which they are parasites; while others are mandibulate, or have mandibles, and also maxillæ, their food consisting of portions of feathers, hairs, and scurf. The legs are usually short and stout, and the claws large and powerful, to enable them to hold firmly to the hairs, &c. The Anoplura are most abundant on dirty and diseased animals.

SUCTOR'IA.—The fourth Order of insects consists of the genus *Púlex,*—*Pulex irrítans* being the human

N 2

flea.   Other species are found upon different animals,
as upon the dog, the rat (Pl. X. fig. 22), the fowl, the
pigeon, &c.

The head and the dark eye (fig. 21, head of the
human flea) are very evident.   The antennæ or head-
feelers are very minute and difficult to find, being
sunk in a little pit or fossa behind the eye; they may,
however, generally be recognized by the detection of
the last joint, which is pectinate or cut like a comb.
The body, including the head, consists of thirteen
joints, one for the head, three for the chest or thorax,
and nine for the belly or abdómen,—it being understood that by "joint" is meant a segment, and not the
line of junction of two segments.   The indication of
these joints is afforded by the horny integument,
which consists of a corresponding number of rings,
forming in fact the skeleton of the animal.   This in
the flea, as in all insects and other Articulata, is external or cutaneous (*cútis*, skin), and consists of the
hardened skin, the peculiar animal substance of which
it is composed being called chitine (χιτὼν, tunic).
These chitinous rings overlap, and are composed of a
dorsal or upper, and a ventral or lower half; and
near the middle of each is a row of hairs directed
backwards.   Along the sides of the body of the insect may be seen a row of dots; these are the spiracles
or orifices of the breathing-tubes (tracheæ).

The legs are many-jointed, long, furnished with
numerous spines, and terminated by two slightly
curved claws, each with a little blunt tooth at its
base.   The claws are not perfectly smooth on the
inside, but are covered with slightly raised lines, like
a file, so that a better hold can be taken of bodies.

But the most interesting parts of the flea are those
of the mouth, with which it punctures the skin and
sucks the blood.   There are nine of these; and they are
best seen when the head of the flea is pulled off with
the mounted needles, and the parts spread out and

mounted in balsam, a high power being used to examine them. One of them forms a long and slender bristle (seta) or tongue, furnished with distant minute teeth. On each side of this is a flattened seta, with two rows of teeth on the edges; these are the lancets, and when not in use these organs are inclosed in two jointed sheaths. Outside these are two representatives of jaws, or maxillæ (b), each having a jointed feeler or palp (a) arising from it; the probable use of the palps being to feel the position of the skin, so that the animal may be able to adjust the lancets at a proper distance for puncture.

The eggs of the flea are often visible within the body of the parent; and when this is crushed, they are more distinctly seen, of various sizes, and contained within a long tube, which is the ovary or egg-bag. The eggs are laid by the animals upon carpets, woollen garments, or in the cracks of dirty floor-boards; they are just perceptible to the eye as white oblong specks, and they may always be found on the rug when a cat is kept in the house. When hatched, they give rise to a minute white worm-like maggot, or larva (fig. 30), having a 12-jointed body, with two rudimentary antennæ and two slightly curved hooks appended to the last joint. The mouth-organs of the larva are adapted for biting, and not for sucking, as in the perfect animal, the jaws or maxillæ being distinctly toothed. When they have acquired full growth, which takes place in about twelve days in warm weather, they spin around themselves a little silky cocoon, and become transformed into a chrysalis or pupa; and from this, in about a fortnight, the perfect insect escapes.

DIP'TERA (δὶς, twice, πτερὸν, wing).—This, which forms the fifth Order of Insects, consists of the two-winged insects, or flies, as the house-fly, the blue-bottle, the gnats, &c.

MUS'CIDÆ.—The house-fly, and the blue-bottle or

meat-fly, are both species of the genus *Mus'ca*, belonging to this family, the former being *Musca domes'tica*, the latter *Musca vomitor'ia*. Both these insects are seen to be wonderfully constructed when minutely examined, and they possess considerable resemblance in general structure.

On examining the head of the house-fly (Pl. X. fig. 17) under a low power, and as an opake object, the observer will be struck with the remarkable appearance presented by the two eyes, which are large, placed one on each side of the fore part of the head, and composed of very numerous little eyes closely packed together, or they are compound, as it is called. The use of this compound structure is evidently to enable the little animal to see in all directions without moving the head and eyes. Each little eye has a lens to bring the rays of light emanating from objects to a focus upon a nerve. The packing of the eyes together gives rise to their angular form or their straight sides, each of the little surfaces or facets being hexagonal, or bounded by six sides (fig. 33). In front of and between the eyes are seen the two small antennæ; these have three joints, the third of which is larger than the rest (fig. 17 *a*), and arising from near its base is a feathery bristle or seta; these structures are best seen when the antennæ are pulled off with a pair of forceps and mounted separately. Below the antennæ, and extending downwards and forwards is the proboscis, or tongue, as it is called, which can be entirely retracted within a pit in the fore part of the head, or protruded at the will of the animal. This is a very beautiful and complicated instrument, and is best examined when spread out and separately mounted (Pl. X. fig. 29). It consists of a fleshy tube, dilated at the end into two lobes, which are flattened beneath to form a sucking-disk. The end is furnished with two solid horny lateral branches to keep it expanded, and with two longitudinal tubes beneath, running parallel, from the outer sides of which arise numerous nearly parallel branches. These tubes and their branches are incomplete beneath, and consist of imperfect rings, otherwise greatly resembling tracheæ. On each side of the proboscis is a lip-feeler or labial palpus, for the organ represents the labium of other insects. All these parts are better seen in the proboscis of the blow-fly than in that of the house-fly, on account of their larger size. The head, the thorax, and the abdomen are very distinct in the fly, being separated from each other by well-marked constrictions.

The legs are composed of five parts, each having a separate name. The first piece or joint, which is that attached to the body, is called the hip, or coxa; the next is a very small, somewhat triangular piece, and is the trochan'ter; next comes the long and stout thigh, or fémur; this being succeeded by the tib'ia, which, as in most insects, is furnished with strong spines at the end; and lastly is the foot, or tar'sus, consisting of five joints, the three last of which are represented in the figure (Pl. X. fig. 32). At the end of the fifth or last joint of the tarsus (fig. 32) (for it must be noted that the joints of the limbs of insects are always numbered in order of distance from the body) are two soft little cushions, or pulvil'li, which are covered on the under surface with numerous hair-like bodies dilated at the end, acting as suckers in enabling the fly to adhere to smooth surfaces. In addition to these organs are two curved claws, and between them a sharp straight spine.

The eggs of the fly are deposited upon heaps of decaying animal and vegetable matters, as dungheaps, &c. The blow-fly deposits its eggs in the same situations, but especially those where the animal matters are most abundant: every one knows the eggs as deposited upon tainted meats, when they are called fly-blows. When the eggs are hatched, the *larvæ* or maggots make their appearance. The larvæ of the blow-fly are well known to the angler, who uses them for bait, and calls them gentles.

These larvæ exhibit some interesting points of structure. The jointed or ringed condition of the body is distinct to the naked eye. The head is provided with two rudimentary palpi, placed each upon a rounded papilla; also with two brown curved and horny hooks or jaws. On the posterior end of the body are two brown spots, which consist of spiracles, and have three sieve-like oblong orifices; and at the anterior margin of each segment of the body are very numerous little short spines, with the points directed backwards. These answer the purpose, to some extent, of legs; for when the larva is moving, and has forced itself through the matter in which it burrows, the little spines prevent the body being forced backwards as the head is pushed forwards and meets any resistance.

To examine the structure of these larvæ, the gentles should be killed by immersion for a time in warm water, and then dried by touching them with blotting-paper. The hooks and palpi can be seen by holding the body in the forceps as an opake object. To observe the spiracles, the end of the body should be cut off, and the animal matter washed away in a watch-glass with water and a hair pencil, then spread out, dried between two slides, and mounted in balsam.

The larvæ of the house-fly and of the blow-fly very closely resemble each other, so much so that the former are generally overlooked; hence it is often wondered where flies come from, although they are so numerous in every house. When the larvæ of these flies are fully developed, they gradually assume a brown colour, the organs of the head are retracted, and the skin becomes dry and hard. This is the state of *pupa*, or chrysalis; and while remaining in this state of rest, the development of the wings, legs,

&c., takes place; so that when the insect emerges from the shell of the chrysalis, it has attained its highest state of development, and forms the *imágo* or perfect insect. It may be remarked here, that when insects pass through the three states of larva, pupa, and imago, they are said to undergo complete metamorphosis. There is not a more curious object than that presented by the young fly contained in its case, as seen on carefully cutting away portions from one end of the case of the chrysalis. The body and head are quite white, with beautiful blood-red eyes.

Most persons must have noticed another kind of house-fly, having the wings more widely separated than in the common fly, and moving more slowly through the air. This is *Stomox'ys cal'citrans.* The proboscis of this fly (Pl. X. fig. 18) differs from that of the house-fly in being longer, more bent, and but little expanded at the end; also in being provided with two long setæ, one forming a slender sharp lancet, the other being somewhat stouter, and forming its sheath. The fly is thus enabled to pierce the flesh and suck the blood.

CULIC'IDÆ.—We will now say a few words about the gnats, which are old favourites for microscopic examination. The three states of larva, pupa, and imago must be considered separately.

The imago or perfect form is well known. The males are easily distinguished from the females by the difference in structure of the antennæ, which in the males (Pl. X. fig. 10, head) are very beautifully plumose or feathery, whilst in the females (fig. 11) the hairs are very short—the long proboscis, or rostrum, or bundle of biting-organs forming the striking feature; this difference is immediately evident to the naked eye.

The antennæ of the males (fig. 10 *a*) consist of numerous small joints, from each of which arises a ring of long hairs, giving the appearance of a tuft on each side when flattened for view as a transparent object under the microscope; at the end are two longer joints, the first having a small ring of shorter hairs.

The proboscis of the female is a very complicated organ, consisting of six separate bristle-like pieces or setæ, all nearly of the same length. Two of these are somewhat curved near the end, and provided on the inside with fine teeth; another pair consists of very thin lancet-pointed instruments; then comes another lancet-pointed seta, very sharp at the end, and traversed by a canal; next, a stouter and darker-looking tube, slit up underneath, which serves to contain the two toothed setæ; and lastly, a stout and broader sheath, also slit up throughout its length beneath, in which all are packed. This sheath has two lobes at the end, and has some resemblance to the proboscis of the fly, of which organ it is the representative.

The gnat lays its eggs in water. The eggs are longish oval, with a kind of neck at the upper end; they are glued together side by side in large numbers, and form a boat-like mass, floating on the surface of the water. The larvæ (Pl. X. fig. 9) are very commonly found skipping through the water, or hanging, as it were, by the tail from the surface. The head is very broad; and arising from each joint of the body are tufts of hairs. Near the end of the body is a tube which communicates with the tracheæ; and when the animal is quiet, this tube is brought to the surface; so that when the animal appears hanging to the surface, it is breathing. In addition to this method of respiration, there are other respiratory organs attached to the last joint of the body, consisting of leaf-like plates; hence these larvæ have an aquatic as well as an aërial respiration: the respiratory or branchial plates also serve as a tail to aid in swimming. Running down the back of the larva will be seen a thin delicate vessel, dilated opposite the thorax, and beating or contracting at regular intervals. This is the dorsal vessel, the dilatation representing the heart of the higher animals; and it serves to propel the colourless blood throughout the body.

After several moultings or castings of the skin, to allow of the growth of the insect (for insects grow only in the larval state), the larva becomes transformed into the pupa (Pl. X. fig. 8). In this state the animals still move about in the water, and are often found suspended from its surface by two respiratory tubes, which, however, are not connected with the tail, but arise from the thorax; and the various parts of the perfect insect may be seen through the case or skin, within which they are closely packed.

When the pupa has attained its full development, the perfect insect emerges from it, leaving the water to fly about and seek food.

Tipu'lidæ.—In the water of ponds and pools a young larva (Pl. X. fig. 31) will often be met with, which is that of *Chiron'omus plumósus,* a largish gnat-like insect, belonging to the daddy-long-legs family (Tipulidæ). This larva exhibits the usual thirteen segments, including the head. In the young state the body is nearly colourless; but in the mature larva it is of a blood-colour, and about an inch in length. Beneath the first joint of the body are two foot-like processes covered with hair; and at the end of the body are also two processes, surmounted with hooks. The three last joints of the body are also furnished each with a pair of fleshy processes, those of the first pair being very short.

Hymenop'tera (ὑμὴν, membrane, πτερὸν, wing).— This, which forms the sixth Order of insects, contains the bee, the wasp, the ant, &c.

In the Hymenoptera there is a curious contrivance for linking the two wings on each side, so that they may form a single piece in the flight of the insect.

It consists of a row of hooks, placed upon the anterior nerve of the hind wing, which play upon the folded-in corresponding edge of the fore wing; the hooks, sliding along this edge, allow of freedom of motion, although still holding the two wings together. This structure may be well seen in the wings of the Humble Bee when mounted in balsam.

The sting of the wasp and bee is also a singular organ. In both insects it is much alike, consisting of a sheath, slit up beneath, in which are contained two long setæ, or lancets, with bent-back (recurved) teeth near the end. These setæ are inserted into the flesh during the act of stinging, and at the same time the poisonous secretion from two glands is forced into the wound, which causes the severe pain resulting from the sting.

In the wingless neuters of the common ant, attached to the end of the tibia (Pl. X. fig. 34 c) is a beautiful pectinate process, somewhat resembling a comb (fig. 34 a).

LEPIDOP'TERA (λεπὶς, scale, πτερὸν, wing).—This Order contains the butterflies and the moths, the entire bodies of which are covered with minute scales. When the insects are handled, these scales adhere to the fingers as a fine dust; and on pressing a slide against the insects, they may be removed for examination. They consist of a very slender and short quill, by which they are attached, and a flattened plate of various forms (Pl. X. fig. 19, b,f); it is, however, generally narrower near the quill, and expanded towards the free end, where it is often cut into lobes or tooth-like segments. The scales are usually covered with continuous longitudinal lines or ridges, with granules of colouring-matter (pigment) situated between the two thin layers of which the scales consist. In some of them the form is that of a filament, either simple or branched at the end (fig. 19 e), when they resemble minute hairs. In the males of the large white Cabbage Butterfly (*Pi'eris brass'icæ*), certain of the scales of the wings are covered with longitudinal rows of very minute dots (fig. 19*f*), and have little tassel-like bodies at the end. The males may be distinguished from the females by the front wings having no black spots, while those of the females have two upon each wing. When the scales are examined as they exist upon the wings of the Lepidoptera, they are found to be imbricated (Pl. X. fig. 3) or overlapping each other like the tiles on the roof of a house.

The Lepidoptera suck the honey of flowers by means of a spiral tongue (Pl. X. fig. 20 *c*) or ant'lia (*antlia*, a sucking-tube); this consists of two halves, which represent the maxillæ of other insects; and their margins are fringed with little tassel-like bodies, probably organs of taste. The antennæ (fig. 20 *a*) are many-jointed, clubbed at the ends (*d*) in the butterflies, and simple in the moths. The palpi (fig. 20 *b*) are short and densely covered with scales. In the large eyes the facets are very distinct and suitable for examination.

The larvæ are well known as caterpillars. They have six legs, as in the perfect insects, but rudimentary and with single claws; also some additional pairs of pro-legs, as they are called, with a crown of hooks, towards the hind part of the body. The spiracles of caterpillars are very favourable for observation.

NEUROP'TERA (*νεῦρον*, nerve, *πτερὸν*, wing).—This Order contains the Dragon-flies (Libellúlidæ), the Day-fly (*Ephem'era*), &c., in which the wings are usually so large and so beautifully netted. The species figured (Pl. X. fig. 1), which is wingless, is very common in old books and in collections of dried plants. It is whitish, mite-like, with setaceous many-jointed antennæ, 3-jointed tarsi, and very broad thighs (femora). Its name is *At'ropos pulsator'ius*.

HEMIP'TERA (*ἥμισυς*, half, *πτερὸν*, wing).—This Order contains the bugs and other noxious insects.

Those which we shall notice are the species of *A'phis*, commonly known as Plant-lice and Green-fly, which are found too frequently upon unhealthy plants. The species figured (Pl. X. fig. 2) is that of the geranium (*Pelargonium*). The head is small and notched or emarginate. The body is oval and furnished behind with two prolonged tubercles, these being covered with scales, giving them a somewhat striated appearance (fig. 2 *b*). The antennæ are 6-jointed (*c*), the second joint being very small, the last joint long, excavated on one side, and ringed: these organs are reflexed over the body in the natural state. There are two compound eyes, and three simple eyes or ocelli, forming a triangle on the top of the head. The proboscis or rostrum is bent under the body, 4-jointed, and contains three setæ, two of them forming very slender lancets. The legs are long; the tarsi (fig. 2 *a*) 2-jointed, the first or basal joint being very minute, and the last furnished with two claws.

In a colony of these insects, some are winged and some wingless; those without wings being usually in the larva state, the pupæ having rudimentary wings, and the males and females usually perfect wings. *Aphis brass'icæ* is the destructive turnip-fly.

COLEOP'TERA (κολεὸς, sheath).—This, which is the last Order to be noticed, contains the Beetles, so easily recognized by their hard and horny fore wings or wing-cases. The parts of the mouth in these insects are exceedingly well adapted for examination; and as they are not fused or consolidated with each other, they serve to illustrate the typical constitution of the organs as existing in these animals.

Pteros'tichus (*Ster'opus*) *mad'idus* (Pl. X. fig. 23) is common in cellars and gardens among vegetable rubbish. The body of this beetle is shining black, the head projecting; the antennæ (fig. 23 *a*) are filiform, and compressed towards the end. The thorax is somewhat rounded, with a deep rough pit and a longitudinal stria at each posterior angle. The wing-cases, or elytra, are longitudinally striated; the wings, which in most beetles are concealed beneath the elytra when the insects are at rest, being absent. The tibiæ of the fore legs are notched on the inside (fig. 24 *a*), a fringe of hairs being situated in the notch; the tarsi are 5-jointed (fig. 24 *b*), the first four joints being triangular, the last elongate and terminated by two curved claws. In the male the three first joints of the tarsi of the anterior legs (fig. 24 *b*) are dilated and heart-shaped.

The parts of the mouth (which are named after an analogy with those of the higher animals) consist of the following pieces:—An upper lip, or *lábrum* (fig. 25 *a*), which is squarish (quad'rate) and slightly notched; a quadrate lower lip, or *lábium* (fig. 27), with a process on each side, and two 4-jointed lip-feelers or labial palpi (*b*); and below the labium is a chin, or *mentum* (fig. 27 *a*), with a projecting bifid tooth: these parts form the roof and the floor of the mouth. Next come the *man'dibles* (fig. 26), one on each side, which are stout, curved, and pointed; beneath which are the *maxil'læ* (fig. 28), also one on each side, and provided with a fixed claw (*a*), ciliated on the in-side, and furnished with two pairs of jaw-feelers, or *maxillary palpi*, the inner (*b*) being 2-jointed, while the outer (*c*) are 4-jointed. It will be noticed that the jaws work laterally, or from side to side, and not perpendicularly as in the higher animals.

These parts may be found in most beetles which the observer may submit to examination, being how-ever somewhat modified in different genera. We may consider those existing in the Lady-birds, or species of *Coccinel'la*, by way of comparison. The body in these insects is very convex, and the head sunk deeply in the thorax. The antennæ (fig. 15) are short, clubbed (clávate), and compressed. The thorax is short and lúnate, or half-moon shaped.

The mandibles (fig. 13) are curved, bifid at the apex, and with a tooth on the inside near the base. The labrum (fig. 14) is transverse, or broader than long. The labium (fig. 12) is furnished with two palpi, which are 3-jointed. The maxillæ (fig. 16) are two-lobed, the lobes (*b, c*) being ciliated, and the 4-jointed palpi (*a*) have the last joint large and hatchet-shaped.

Coleopterous insects undergo complete metamorphosis, the larvæ being commonly known as grubs. The larvæ of the aquatic beetles will often be met with in the water of ponds or ditches, especially that of the common large water-beetle (*Dytis'cus marginális*), or water-boatman as it is called (Pl. X. fig. 7), and in various stages of growth. The structure of the mouth-organs (fig. 6), which are, however, imperfect or rudimentary in some parts, can be readily made out; and their names may easily be found by comparison with what has been stated in regard to the organs of the perfect beetle.

Examination, &c.—The means of catching insects will readily occur to the reader. A bag-net made of a curved piece of cane, to which is fitted a bag made of net, will serve to catch those which trust to flight for escape from their enemies, such as the Lepidoptera; and these may be killed by firm pressure of the thorax between the finger and the thumb. The running insects, as the beetles, may be caught in a spoon or with forceps; and they may be killed by immersion in boiling water or in camphorated spirit. In an excursion, most insects may be carried in a well-corked bottle containing a little wool and a lump of camphor, which stupifies them. When the insects are dead, the limbs should be extended into the natural position by means of pins, the insect being transfixed by a pin run through the thorax or one of the elytra and extending into a sheet of cork. To preserve them, they may be kept in a box, the bottom of which is covered with sheet cork, into which the pins are stuck.

The smaller beetles, &c., which cannot be trans-fixed with a pin, may be mounted as opake objects upon slips of card, the legs &c., being carefully spread out, and gummed in position with a strong solution of gum-tragacanth in boiling water. Many of the smaller Curculion'idæ or diamond-beetles, in which the labium forms a rostrum or beak, with elbowed or half-bent antennæ, form beautiful opake objects when thus mounted, on account of the brilliant scales with which they are covered.

There are two ways of examining insects—either in the entire state as opake objects or the separate parts mounted as transparent objects. In the former case the pin with which the insect is transfixed should be stuck into a slide made of cork, and this laid upon the stage, or the pin may be held by the forceps. In this way, with the use of the side condenser and a low power, the general form and arrangement of the parts of the insect can be made out. The more minute details must be searched for in the individual organs which have been picked off with forceps, and mounted in balsam.

If it be required to submit the parts of a dried insect to examination, this must be previously soaked in warm water for a time, as the legs, &c., become very brittle when dry, and are thus easily injured.

Rotator'ia (*róta*, a wheel) or Rotif'era (*rota* and *fero*, to bear).—The animals contained in this class are minute, being just distinguishable to the naked eye as white specks. They are common in long-kept infusions and among *Confervæ* in the water of pools and ditches. Their body is usually longer than broad, often presenting indications of rings; and at or near the posterior end is frequently found a prolongation resembling a tail, but terminated by two short move-able thumb-like processes, rarely a sucker, which enable the animals to cling to objects. The most characteristic organ, however, is a kind of rounded or oval disk, placed at the anterior end of the body, and furnished with cilia. When these are in active motion, the organ appears as a revolving wheel, whence the name of Wheel-animalcules, by which they are sometimes designated. The wheel-organ enables the animals to swim through the water, and also brings their food to the mouth by the currents which it produces. It is usually cleft into two or more lobes, and can be retracted, as is commonly the case when the animals are disturbed.

In many of these animals the body is more or less covered by a horny shell or carapace; and in some it is fixed at the bottom of a tube, within which it can be withdrawn. On the anterior part of the body are frequently seen two or more red spots, which represent eyes. The alimentary canal is mostly distinct, being indicated by the colour of its contents, and it is lined with cilia. Towards its front portion is a gizzard (Pl. XI. fig. 2 *a*) containing teeth, which are sometimes attached to a jointed jaw-like framework; these are usually in active motion. No heart or blood-vessels have been observed in the Rotatoria; but on each side of the body in many of them is a long wavy tube, containing at intervals minute ciliated bodies, the cilia propelling the water through the tubes, and so exerting an aërating or respiratory function. The reproduction of the Rotatoria takes place by the formation of ova, which may often be distinguished within the body of the parent.

Rotifer vulgáris (Pl. XI. fig. 2) is a common species. It has a spindle-shaped body, which is capable of contraction almost into a ball. The front or head end is sometimes protruded (fig. 2), at others retracted and obscured by the exserted disk (fig. 2*); and beneath it is a tentacle-like organ, supposed to represent an antenna (fig. 2 *b*). The position of the jaws

PLATE XI. [PAGE 150.]

ROTATORIA, INFUSORIA, &c.

Fig.

1. *Anguillula (Dorylaimus)*, species of.
2. *Rotifer vulgaris*: *a*, jaws and teeth; *b*, antenna; 2*, wheel-organ expanded.
3. *Pterodina patina*.
4. *Floscularia ornata*.
5. *Hydra viridis*.
6. *Arcella vulgaris*.
7. *Arcella aculeata*.
8. *Arcella aculeata*, shell with animal.
9. *Arcella dentata*.
10. *Amœba diffluens*.
12. *Actinophrys sol*.
13. Sponge, fibres of; 13 *a, b, c*, spicules of Sponge.
14. *Sertularia pumila*, polypidom.
15. *Sertularia pumila*, polypidom with polypes.
16. *Monas lens*.
17. *Cercomonas globulus*.
18. *Cercomonas crassicauda*.
19. *Heteromita ovata*.
20. *Anthophysa Mülleri*.
21. *Dinobryon sertularia*.
22. *Trachelomonas volvocina*.
23. *Chætoglena volvocina*.
24. *Euglena viridis*.

Fig.

25. *Astasia hæmatodes*.
26. *Enchelys nodulosa*; *a*, undergoing transverse division.
27. *Oxytricha gibba*; 27 *a*, side view.
28. *Paramecium aurelia*: *a*, contractile vesicle; *b*, a gastric sacculus.
29. *Amphileptus fasciola*.
30. *Colpoda cucullus*: *a*, contractile vesicle.
31. *Nassula elegans*: *a*, vesicle; 31 *b*, encysted form.
32. *Coleps hirtus*.
33. *Vaginicola crystallina*.
34. *Vorticella convallaria*: *a*, stalk spirally contracted; *b*, body undergoing longitudinal division.
35. *Vorticella convallaria* encysted and discharging the young brood.
36. *Vorticella convallaria*, body with nucleus (*a*).
37. *Chilodon cucullulus*.
38. *Stentor polymorphus*: *a*, body extended; *b*, body contracted; *c*, bodies aggregated around a globule of jelly; *d*, bodies adherent to the side of a glass.
39. *Alyscum saltans*.
40. *Podophrya fixa*, or the *Podophrya*-form of *Vorticella*.

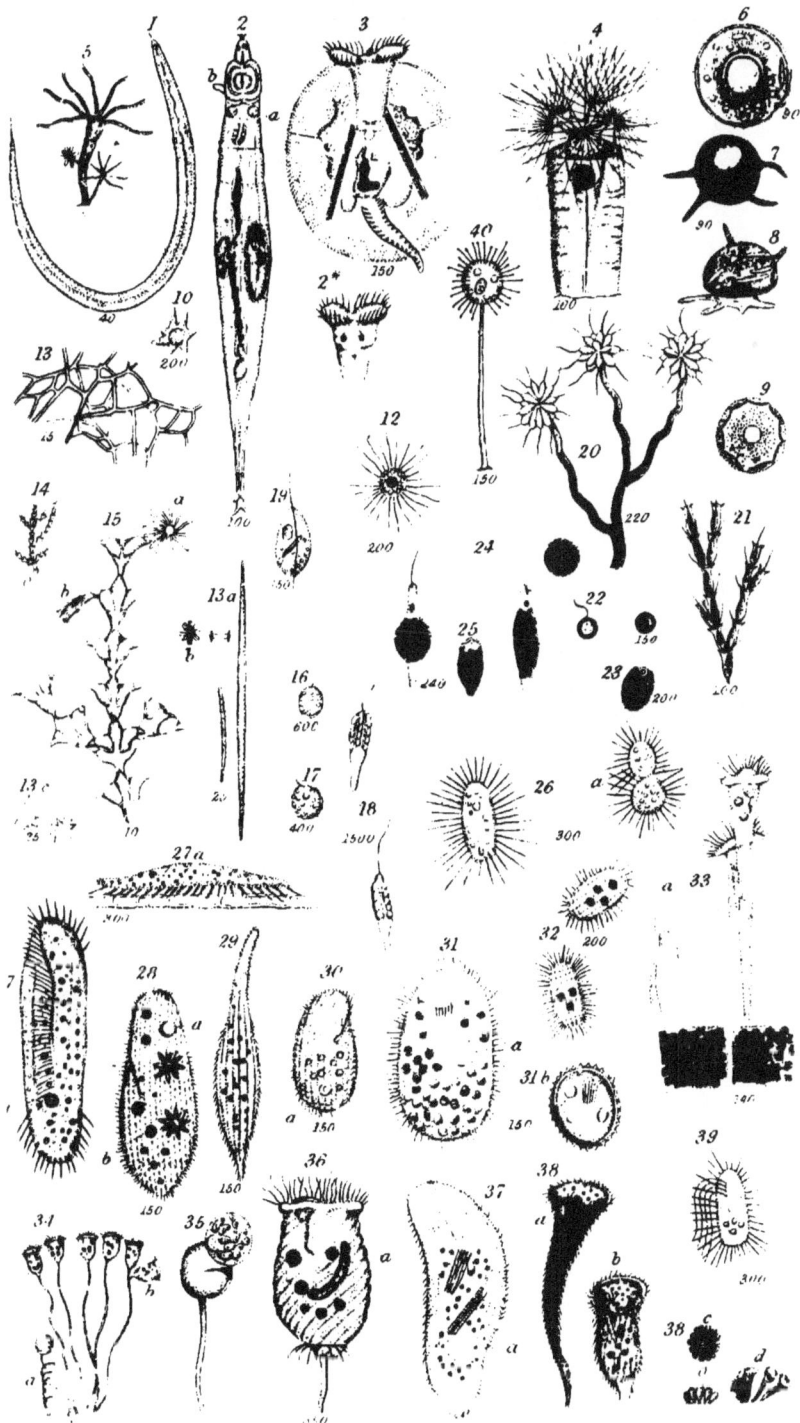

is indicated at *a*. The alimentary canal is seen runing down the body; and two ova exist, one on each side of it, these being often recognizable by the existence of the eyes and jaws. At the end of the body are two lateral processes, and a tail-like piece, which can be withdrawn or protruded and is furnished with two moveable portions or toes.

Pterodína pat'ina (Pl. XI. fig. 3).—This species has a shell or carapace on the back, a two-lobed rotatory organ, two eyes, and a slender wrinkled tail ciliated at the extremity. The curved alimentary canal, and the two strong muscles inclined at an angle, are easily distinguishable.

Flosculária ornáta (Pl. XI. fig. 4) is a very beautiful member of the Rotatoria, and is found adhering to *Confervæ* and other water-plants. The body is club-shaped, and contained in a transparent tube, the ringed narrower portion being fixed to its base. The rotatory organ is divided into five or six lobes, furnished with long, slender, radiating tentacular filaments; these are not vibratile like ordinary cilia, but can be slowly moved. In the contracted state, the filaments form a pencil-like bundle.

Examination, &c.—The Rotatoria are best examined in the living state, the drop of water in which they are viewed being very small, so that their movements may be impeded; and while they are struggling to escape, the various parts of the body will come into view. Their preservation has been attempted by drying on a slide; but when dead they become so contracted and altered, that it is difficult to make out their structure. Should the observer wish to record any observations on their reproduction or habits, it will be well to preserve a specimen of the jaws and teeth, as the species might be with certainty identified by careful examination of their minute structure.

Entozóa (ἐντὸς, within, ζῶον, animal).—This class

consists of the parasitic worms, as the Tape-worm (*Tænia*), the Thread-worm and Round-worm (*As'-caris*), which live within the bodies of man and animals. It also includes the microscopic eel-like animalcules (species of *Anguil'lula*) which are found in sour paste (*A. glútinis*), in vinegar (*A. acéti*), and in blighted wheat (*A. trit'ici*). Some of the species of allied genera are met with in damp moss and in the débris or fragments of vegetable substances decaying in water. The general appearance of the microscopic species is that of a minute colourless eel, writhing in the water (Pl. XI. fig. 1). Their internal organs are difficult to distinguish. The alimentary canal is usually evident, and dilated into a kind of stomach, containing near its commencement some rod-like or otherwise-formed teeth. In the species figured there are two apparently tubular lancets, which are capable of protrusion, and evidently serve to wound the prey.

CHAPTER XII.

RADIATA.

DESCENDING in the scale of animal organization, we come next to the subkingdom RADIÁTA, or that in which the parts are arranged in a radiate manner around a centre. Of this there are three classes,—the ECHINODER′MATA (ἐχῖνος, hedgehog, δέρμα, skin), containing the Sea-urchins (*Echínus*), Starfishes, &c., in which the skin is furnished with hard calcareous projecting spines or curiously formed imbedded calcareous corpuscles, forming a rudimentary skeleton; the ACALÉPHÆ (ἀκαλήφη, a nettle), or Sea-nettles; and the POL′YPI (πολὺς, many, ποῦς, foot), to which we shall confine our notice. It may be remarked that the last two classes have recently been united to form the single class CŒLENTERÁTA (κοῖλον, hollow, ἔντερον, intestine).

POLYPI.—These animals are mostly marine. They are either single (Pl. XI. fig. 5), or compound (Pl. XI. fig. 15), *i.e.* the bodies are united; in the latter case the bodies being usually situated in horny cells upon a branched polypidom. But in many of them, which do not occur in this country, there is an internal solid calcareous skeleton, of which coral is an example. The animal bodies are soft, and furnished at the front end with a crown of tentacles (fig. 15 *a*); these are contractile, and serve to enable the animals to catch their prey. The horny, branched, and plant-like polypidoms are often found on the seashore, and are popularly confounded with sea-weeds.

Hy′dra vulgáris (Pl. XI. fig. 5) is a fresh-water species, which is commonly met with among collections of water-plants, and may generally be obtained by collecting some of these and placing them in a glass jar of fresh water. When the water has stood for some hours, the Polypes will be seen, on careful examination, adhering to the sides of the glass. The body of the animals is cylindrical, hollow, and furnished with from six to ten tentacles, arranged in a circle, in the centre of which is the mouth. The tentacles are hollow, and communicate with the cavity of the body. On examination with a high power, the tentacles will be found to exhibit minute oval sacs, containing a long fibre coiled up within them; and when the tentacles are touched by any foreign body, the fibres are suddenly discharged. These are the stinging or urticating organs. The *Hydræ* move very slowly; but the body is very contractile, and is often seen of various forms. When a minute animal, as an Entomostracan, happens to come into contact with the tentacles, these curve around it, holding it firmly, and finally bringing it to the mouth. It is then forced into the cavity of the body of the animal, where it is digested, the remains being discharged at the mouth. The movements of the *Hydra*, when devouring its prey, form a very curious and interesting spectacle. The *Hydræ* are propagated by budding or gemmation, also by the formation of capsules in the walls of the body, containing ova and spermatozoa. The young Polypes formed by budding are represented in the figure, adhering to the base of the parent.

Sertulária púmila (Pl. XI. fig. 15) is a marine species, the polypidom being frequently found adhering to *Fuci* and other sea-weeds; it is about half an inch long. The cells are opposite, pointed at the ends, and with an oblique orifice. The tentacles are fourteen in this species. In the summer large ovate cells are found, arising from the polypidom; these contain the eggs, and are called ovisacs or ovig'erous vesicles.

CHAPTER XIII.

PROTOZÓA (πρῶτος, FIRST, ζῶον, ANIMAL).

THE members of this subkingdom are the lowest in the scale of animal organization, their bodies consisting of a soft gelatinous and structureless mass, which has a remarkable tendency to form little cavities or vacuoles in its substance, and is called *sar'code* (σάρξ, flesh). They exhibit no organs, unless the cilia and certain variable processes formed of the common substance of the body, and which form their agents of locomotion, be considered as such,—this substance exercising the combined functions of motion, sensation, and secretion, for which separate organs exist in the higher animals.

RHIZOP'ODA (ῥίζα, root, πούς, foot).—The animals belonging to this class consist of the structureless colourless substance to which reference has been made as sarcode, and they exhibit no organs. The sarcodic body is slowly contractile, and portions of it can be protruded at will in the form of irregular root-like processes, acting both as legs for locomotion and as tentacles by which the animal grasps its prey, which is then forced into the substance of the body, where it becomes surrounded by the surface, and a cavity is formed, within which it is digested.

Amœ'ba diffluens (Pl. XI. fig. 10) is common in water in which portions of plants have been kept for some time. When first placed on the slide, the body appears as a minute, transparent, rounded mass of jelly; but if observed for some time, it will be seen slowly to protrude its root-like processes ; and foreign bodies, as Diatomaceæ or other minute Algæ, will often be found imbedded in its substance.

Arcella vulgáris (Pl. XI. fig. 6) is found among *Confervæ* in ponds and ditch-water. It is contained in a hemispherical shell or carapace, from the round orifice of which the lobed processes are protruded. The shell is covered with minute pits.

Arcella aculeáta (Pl. XI. fig. 7) has the convex shell furnished with spines; fig. 8 represents the animal with its processes extended ; while *Arcella dentáta* (Pl. XI. fig. 9) exhibits an angular or some-what toothed membranous shell. Both the latter species are met with in the same localities as the first.

Actínophrys sol (Pl. XI. fig. 12) is a very beautiful and excessively delicate Rhizopod. The body is spherical, and covered with very delicate and slender cilia-like processes. Its movements are exceedingly slow, and can only be observed by prolonged watch-ing. The body appears to be reticulated, from the presence of numerous vacuoles.

Two large groups of genera and species of Rhizo-poda, the animal bodies possessing the above general characters, mostly with very slender processes, exist, in one of which (the FORAMINIFERA) they are con-tained in calcareous shells, often of elegant forms; while in the other (the POLYCYSTINA) the shells are siliceous or composed of flint, both kinds of shells being perforated with holes. These shells, which occur in the fossil state in enormous numbers, sometimes forming mountain-masses, are extremely beautiful objects for the microscope.

SPON'GIÆ.—This class contains the Sponges, almost all of which are marine and foreign, and therefore not likely to come under observation in the per-fect state. The substance commonly called sponge is the horny skeleton of the animal, consisting usually of rounded fibres (Pl. XI. fig. 13), irregularly netted and interlacing. The surface of a sponge exhibits minute pores and larger pouting orifices; the former of which admit currents of water, to be discharged at the latter, both being the mouths of continuous channels. The surfaces of the channels are lined with sarcodic matter, which takes the form of ciliated amœbiform bodies, by which the currents of liquid are produced.

The horny fibres of sponges are strengthened by little siliceous or flinty bodies of various forms (Pl. XI. fig. 13 a, b, c), which are imbedded in the substance of the fibres or attached to their surface, and form very curious microscopic objects. They are called *spic'ula* (*spiculum*, a dart), being often of a pointed form. In some sponges they are calcareous.

INFUSOR'IA.—The animals contained in this class are usually very minute, being rarely even perceptible to the naked eye, except when existing in very large numbers, so as to render the water milky, green, or red. They are found in all kinds of water, but especially in stagnant pools and in decomposing solutions or infusions of vegetable matters. The true structure of their bodies is a matter of doubt, some authors having considered them as being highly organized, while others have regarded them as consisting of simple cells; and whether they are correctly referred to the Protozoa must remain at present a matter of doubt. The body is of various forms, as represented in Plate XI. figs. 16–40. In some of them it consists of a simple sarcodic mass, evidently without any outer skin, as shown by its ready adhesion and laceration on accidental contact with foreign bodies; while in others the surface is regularly dotted with little depressions, or with nodules, so as to resemble a definitely organized structure.

The most striking character of the Infusoria is the presence of vibratile cilia, which are variously ar-

P

ranged; in some entirely covering the body, irregularly or in regular rows, in others being situated at definite parts only. By the action of the cilia they are enabled to swim freely in the water, also to obtain their food, which consists of minute Algæ or fragments of animal matter. In many of them there is a special row or set of cilia, which, by the currents it produces, urges the particles of food suspended in the water towards the mouth. The cilia also act as respiratory organs, by changing the water with which their bodies are in contact. In some of the species there are stout bristles or setæ, by which they are enabled to crawl upon water-plants.

On carefully examining the bodies of the Infusoria, rounded granular spots will be seen, frequently containing minute Algæ, &c. (fig. 28 *b*). These spots are the digestive cavities, and have been called *gastric sac'culi*; but whether they are definite sacs or mere excavations, formed by the particles of food having been forced into the softer internal substance of the body, has not been positively determined. The sacculi may be filled artificially by mixing very fine indigo, or carmine, on a slide with the water in which the Infusoria are contained. A definite food-tube or alimentary canal has been detected in a few of the Infusoria; but it cannot be shown to exist in the majority of them.

A mouth exists in most of them, and is sometimes indicated by a row or set of cilia somewhat larger than those existing upon other parts of the body, and leading to or placed near it. The particles of food which have entered the body are often seen to pass round it, as if circulating, descending on one side and ascending on the other.

In addition to the gastric sacculi, certain clear transparent spots may also be seen within the body, appearing light or dark according to the adjustment of the focus. If these are attentively watched, they will be seen to contract and finally disappear, becoming again distended and vanishing at tolerably regular intervals. These are the *contractile vesicles* (figs. 27 *a*, 28 *a*, 37 *a*), and they contain a clear liquid, the nature of which is uncertain.

In many of the Infusoria is a round or elongate granular body (figs. 31 *a*, 36 *a*), which is called the nucleus, the term having been applied to it from a notion that the Infusoria consisted of simple cells. A minute red spot is also often seen at the anterior end of the body, which is supposed to represent an eye, and is called an eye-spot. The Infusoria are propagated in several ways :—by budding or gemmation, new beings sprouting out in a bud-like form, usually from the base of the parent; by division, either transverse (fig. 26 *a*) or longitudinal (fig. 34 *b*), of the body gradually into two parts, each of which subsequently becomes a perfect animal; by encysting, the body contracting into a globular form, and forming a firm coat around it, the contents becoming resolved into a numerous progeny of young; and by conjugation and the agency of spermatozoa and ova. We will now proceed to the examination of a few species, arranging them in the order of the families to which they belong.

MONAD'INA.—In this family the bodies of the Infusoria are very soft, and without a skin or integument; they are also exceedingly minute, and will not admit the particles of indigo.

Mon'as lens (Pl. XI. fig. 16) is very minute, and commonly found in old infusions. Its body is rounded and flattened, and granular on the surface. At the front end of the body is a whip-like or flagel'liform (*flagel'lum*, a whip) filament, differing from a cilium in being rigid at the base and moveable at the end only, by which it is enabled to row itself through the water with a wriggling motion.

Cercom'onas glob'ulus (fig. 17) has a spherical body,

with two flagelliform filaments, one arising from the front, the other from the end of the body. In *Cercomonas crassicau'da* (fig. 18) the posterior filament is replaced by a tail-like narrowing of the body.

Heterom'ita ováta (fig. 19) has the body ovate, with two long anterior flagelliform filaments, one of which is directed forwards, while the other trails behind.

Anthophy'sa mül'leri (fig. 20) has the monad bodies arranged in little heads at the ends of an irregularly branched brown stalk. After a time they become detached and revolve freely in the water.

DINOBRY'INA.—*Dinobry'on sertuláira* (Pl. XI. fig. 21) forms a minute Sertularia-like polypidom, consisting of rows of cells, each containing an oval monad with a single anterior filament. The two last species are common in bog-water.

THECAMONAD'INA.—In these Infusoria the body is inclosed in a firm and sometimes brittle shell or carapace.

Trachelom'onas volvoc'ina (Pl. XI. fig. 22) has a spherical red shell, the body being furnished with a single filament and a minute red eye-spot; while *Chætogléna volvoc'ina* (fig. 23) has an oblong shell, covered with little spines.

EUGLÉNIA.—In this family the form of the body is constantly changing, being at one time spherical, at another fusiform or ovate. It is covered with a contractile skin or firmer external portion, and has one or more flagelliform filaments for locomotion. The species are common in stagnant pools, often colouring the water green or red.

Eugléna vir'idis (Pl. XI. fig. 24) has a spindle-shaped body when fully expanded, the ends being pale; and at the front end is a red eye-spot.

Astásia hæmatódes (fig. 25), which is probably a form of the *Euglena*, is found in stagnant pools, which it renders red. It has no eye-spot.

ENCHÉLIA.—These Infusoria are found in stagnant water and in decomposing infusions. The body is covered with cilia variously arranged, but there is no integument nor mouth.

En'chelys nodulósa (Pl. XI. fig. 26) has a colourless, oblong, irregularly nodular body, coated with very slender radiating cilia, and often exhibits numerous vacuoles. It is frequently found undergoing transverse division (fig. 26 *a*), the body becoming gradually constricted until it separates into two parts, which become perfect animals.

Alys'cum sal'tans (fig. 39) has an ovoid-oblong, slightly furrowed body, surrounded with radiating cilia, and has a side bundle of long retractile cilia, by means of which it leaps from place to place in the water.

KERÓNIA.—In this family the body is soft, irregularly ciliated, without a special integument, but has an oblique row of vibratile cilia leading to the mouth, and stouter cilia or bristles (setæ) on certain parts of the body. The sacculi often contain Diatomaceæ, &c.

Oxyt'richa gib'ba (Pl. XI. fig. 27) has a colourless, oblong body, somewhat expanded in the middle, with setæ at the two ends. In the side view (fig. 27 *a*), the body is seen to be convex above and flattened beneath.

PARAMEC'INA.—The species belonging to this family have a soft, flexible body, which is usually oblong and flattened beneath, with an integument covered regularly with pits and rows of cilia.

Col'poda cucul'lus (Pl. XI. fig. 30) has a slightly compressed body, ciliated all over, and kidney-shaped or rounded on one side and notched on the other, the surface exhibiting rows of nodules. The mouth is situated at the bottom of the notch.

Paramécium aurélia (fig. 28) has the body oblong or oblong-ovate, the mouth being placed near the anterior third of its under part. This infusorium is of comparatively large size, and is often found in immense numbers in infusions, which it renders milky. It is admirably adapted for showing the sacculi, which are easily filled with indigo. The body exhibits two remarkable stellate organs, consisting of a central contractile vesicle, surrounded by several radiately placed oval vesicles, which may be seen to contract and dilate with great regularity. The body is coated with very fine cilia.

Amphilep'tus fasciola (fig. 29) is furnished with an elongate fusiform or lanceolate flattened body, with a lateral oblique mouth.

Chil'odon cucul'lulus (fig. 37) has an oblong thin body, irregularly wavy on the sides; the mouth being situated obliquely in front of the middle, and furnished with a cylinder of parallel rod-like teeth.

Nas'sula el'egans (fig. 31) has the body ovoid or oblong, becoming globular when contracted, the mouth being furnished with teeth as in *Chilodon*. It is often found among Oscillatoriæ.

URCEOLARÍNA.—*Vorticel'la convallária* (Pl. XI. fig. 34) is very commonly met with in decomposing infusions. The bell-shaped body is fixed at the end of a slender stalk, which is often seen to be extended and then suddenly contracted into a spiral (fig. 34 *a*). The cilia are arranged around a raised rim at the front of the body, and extend down a fissure leading to the mouth. The sacculi of this infusorium may be readily filled with indigo. The process of longitudinal division may also often be observed, taking about an hour for its completion; and when the new individual is about to separate from the parent, a ring of cilia may be noticed to have sprung up around the base (fig. 36). The encysting process is also often visible, the cilia disappearing, and the body becoming globular and secreting a cyst around it; after a time the contents become resolved into a number of embryos, which escape by the bursting of the cyst (fig. 35). In some cases the *Vorticella* assumes the form of a *Podoph'rya* (fig. 40), the surface becoming covered with tentacle-like processes. This *Podophrya* was formerly considered a distinct species.

Vaginic'ola crystal'lina (fig. 33) is contained in a crystalline tube, from which the body can be protruded. The body is of variable form, presenting when fully extended a trumpet shape. The cilia exist at the anterior end, and extend down a lateral fissure as in *Vorticella*. It is found attached to Confervæ in the water of ponds and bog-pools.

Sten'tor polymor'phus (fig. 38) is a very beautiful trumpet-shaped infusorium, the body being covered with spiral rows of cilia. The rim is furnished with stouter cilia, its margins at the notch being spirally turned inwards. This infusorium is often found in little groups attached to a gelatinous mass (fig. 38 *c*); and it is met with also in a free or unattached state.

COLEP'INA.—*Côleps hir'tus* (fig. 32) has a barrel-shaped carapace, transversely and longitudinally furrowed, the furrows being occupied by cilia. It has two or three spines behind, and ten or twelve at the front end of the carapace. It is common among Confervæ, and is very voracious, feeding upon dead Entomostraca, &c.; and if disturbed at its meal by moving the cover, it will soon return and resume feeding as before.

Examination.—The Infusoria must be examined during life; for they are so altered by preservative liquids that they cannot be well preserved. The shells of those that are provided with them may be kept simply dried upon a slide, and in this way a few will retain their form, and the cilia of all may be more easily distinguished; the vacuoles may also then be seen very distinctly. When they are confined in a small quantity of water and are about to die, a curious phenomenon may be observed in them, a number of oil-like sarcodic globules exuding from the body, and within these, vacuoles may often be seen to form spontaneously.

The Infusoria may be collected in small phials; but it is difficult to keep them, as they form the food of the Entomostraca, the Rotatoria, and the larvæ of insects; so that their enemies are very numerous, and they soon disappear.

CLASSIFICATION.—Before leaving the subject of living bodies, it may be well to make a few remarks upon their systematic relation as defined by classification.

All natural bodies are referable to one of three great kingdoms, viz. the Animal, the Vegetable, or the Mineral Kingdom. The bodies belonging to the latter seldom come under the notice of the microscopic observer, as they are mostly visible to the naked eye, and their minute structure is the same as that of the larger masses. The general structure of the members of the vegetable and animal kingdoms has been illustrated in the preceding pages. These bodies are distinguished from those of the mineral kingdom by their vital power of appropriating surrounding matters to their own nutrition and growth—this power being exercised by their organs, or, in the lowest forms, by any portion of their substance. Hence animals and vegetables or plants are termed organic bodies, while minerals are termed inorganic bodies, as having no organs; and the material of which organic bodies consist is termed organic matter, that of minerals being inorganic matter. But in both animals and plants inorganic matter is mixed with the organic matter, having been taken up or absorbed from the inorganic kingdom, although it does not usually exist in its characteristic condition, which is that of crystals, i. e. angular solids, as crystals of Epsom salts, &c. The individual members of the

animal and vegetable kingdoms are systematically
divided into certain groups, and these into successively
smaller groups until we arrive at the species. These
groups are founded upon the possession of certain
points of resemblance by their members, forming the
distinguishing characters, and their names are signi-
ficant and definite. They usually run as follows, the
larger and higher groups standing first in order :—
Kingdoms, Subkingdoms, Classes, Orders, Families,
Tribes, Genera, and Species. But it must be observed
that the term species has a different value from that
of the other terms ; for the individuals of which the
species consist are not only related by resemblance
of structure, but also by their origin—being supposed
to have derived their origin from a parent of original
creation ; while the other groups have, as far as we
know, no other relation than that of similarity of
structure.

It is obvious that the characters of the various
groups might be founded upon peculiarities of any
kind. But on this point two methods must be specially distinguished, in one of which the groups are
founded upon the sum of all the peculiarities, while
in the other they are based upon the structure of
single parts or organs. In the former case the system
is called natural, in the latter artificial. And while the
latter often brings together beings which have per-
haps but one or two points of resemblance, and separates others which are closely related, the former
associates those which are really and naturally similar.

All the groups have special names, so that they
may be referred to and spoken of as in the case of
common things ; the names being composed of Greek
or Latin words, so that they may be intelligible to all
nations ; and as these are dead languages, they will
remain good for all time.

In mentioning the name of an animal or plant, the
name of the genus is always used with that of the

species; thus, the name of Chickweed is *Stellaria media*. Because there are mostly several species in a genus; so that if the name of the genus only were used, the species meant would be uncertain; and as there are often species of the same name in different genera, if the name of the species only were used, the genus meant would be doubtful.

The classification of animals and plants serves two important purposes : one is that the structural peculiarities and affinities of the groups may be contrasted and a knowledge of their absolute and their differential characters acquired, and for this a natural system is eminently serviceable; the second is that of enabling any animal or plant to be simply distinguished from any other, for which an artificial or analytical system is extremely useful.

CHAPTER XIV.

OPTICAL PRINCIPLES.

We shall now devote a few pages to the consideration of the nature of light, and the optical principles involved in the construction and use of the microscope. Two theories of light have been propounded. According to one, light consists of minute particles emanating from self-luminous bodies, as the sun, a candle, or a red-hot piece of iron; this is called the corpuscular theory. According to the other, light consists of waves or undulations like those of water or the ears of corn set in motion by the wind, of the molecules of an extremely subtle and rarified elastic matter, called ether, existing everywhere, and set in motion by the causes which produce light; this is called the undulatory theory. The consideration of the merits of these two theories would be foreign to our purpose: suffice it to say that the evidence in favour of the undulatory theory preponderates, so that the corpuscular theory is now laid aside.

It will often be requisite to make use of the term ray of light, by which must be understood the smallest bundle of luminous undulations which can be separated from a mass of light—as by passing light through a small hole in an opake body, or by any equivalent method.

The most casual observer must have noticed that the rays of light move in straight lines, as when the sun's rays are seen entering a dark room through a small window or other aperture, their direction being then distinctly visible; the manner in which ordinary shadows are formed also illustrates the same fact.

Refraction.—But when the rays in their passage impinge or are incident upon and enter a transparent medium or material, of a different density from that which they were at first traversing, their course becomes altered, and the line of their direction broken, whence they are said to be refracted. If the medium upon which the rays impinge be denser than that through which they were at first passing, they will be refracted towards a line perpendicular to the surface, or they will be refracted towards the perpendicular, as it is expressed.

Thus, as shown in Pl. XII. fig. 1, the incident ray *i*, entering the plate of glass, will be refracted at its surface in the direction *a r*, towards the line *p*, which is perpendicular to the surface.

The extent to which the rays undergo refraction depends upon the degree of density of the medium, and varies in the case of each individual substance; but it follows a definite law. If, as in Pl. XII. fig. 2, a circle be drawn around the point *b*, at which the ray *a* is incident, *b r* representing the refracted ray, the lines *s i* and *t r*, drawn at right angles to the perpendicular *p*, will form respectively the sines, as they are called, of the angles *s b i* and *t b r*; *s i* being the sine of the angle of incidence *s b i*, or the angle formed by the incident ray with the perpendicular, and *t r* the sine of the angle of refraction *t b r*, or of that formed by the refracted ray with the perpendicular. These sines, for brevity, are called the sines of incidence and of refraction; and they bear a constant ratio or proportion to each other. Taking the sine of refraction as the unit, or as $=1$, the value of the sine of incidence represents the refractive index or the refractive power of the medium for a ray entering the medium from a vacuum; or, the refractive power of air being extremely small, the value of the sine of incidence may be considered as representing the refractive power from air into the medium.

PLATE XII. [PAGE 168.]

OPTICAL PRINCIPLES.

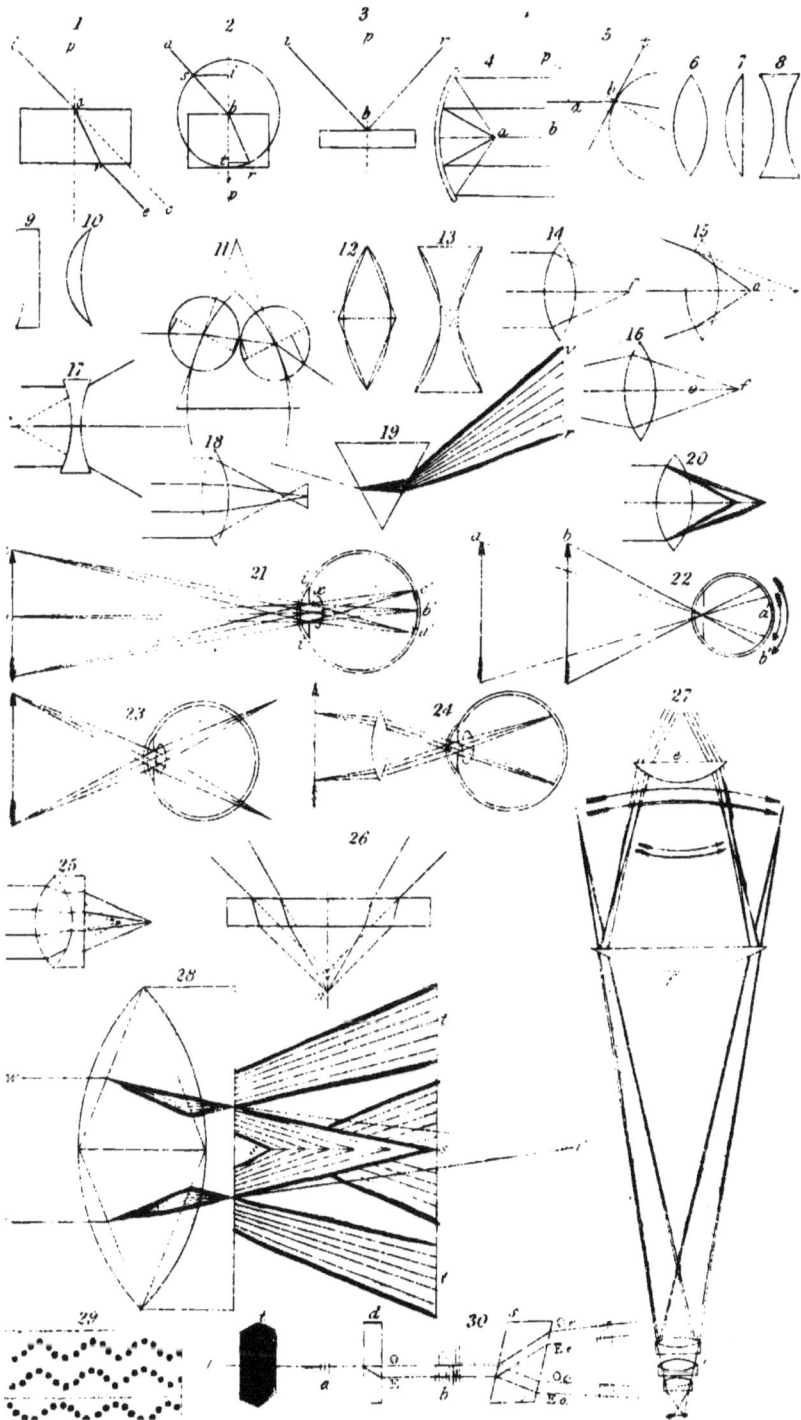

Although the ratio of the sines is constant, the refractive index varies in different media. Thus that of air is 1·0003; of water, 1·336; of Canada balsam, 1·549; of crown glass, from which window-panes are made, 1·535; of flint glass, from which bottles are made, 1·6; of Faraday's heavy glass, composed of silicated borate of lead, 1·8; and of that consisting of borate of lead, 2·0.

A knowledge of this "law of the sines" is of practical importance in determining the direction which the rays will pursue when transmitted through glass lenses, &c. the refractive index of which is known; or in ascertaining the curve which should be given to their surfaces for producing a particular refraction and focal length. Thus, supposing the plate of glass in Pl. I. fig. 2 to consist of crown glass, the refractive index of which is 1·5, the length of the sine of refraction, $t\,r$, will be equal to one part or dimension, while the sine of incidence, $s\,i$, is equal to one part and a half.

It must be remarked that when light is incident at a right angle to the surface of the medium, no refraction takes place, the transmitted ray pursuing its original course.

When a ray of light leaves a denser medium, such as glass, to enter a rarer medium, such as air, it becomes refracted from the perpendicular. In such case, the angle of refraction being greater than the angle of incidence, its sine will also be greater than that of the latter; but the ratio is still preserved.

Reflexion.—When rays of light fall upon a plane surface, as the flat surface of the mirror, a greater or less number of them are reflected, and this according to a definite law, by which the angle of incidence, or that formed by the incident ray with the perpendicular, is equal to the angle of reflexion, or that formed by the reflected ray with the same. Thus, as shown in Pl. XII. fig. 3, the angle $i\,b\,p$, formed by

the incident ray ib with the perpendicular p, is equal
to the angle pbr, formed by the reflected ray br
with the perpendicular pb.

If the body upon the surface of which the rays are
incident be transparent, some of the rays will be refracted and will pass through it, whilst others will be
reflected. The proportion of those reflected is smallest when the rays are incident perpendicularly to the
surface; but this increases as the incident rays become more oblique, $i.\ e.$ as the angle of incidence becomes greater, although at no degree of obliquity are
the whole of the rays reflected. The case is different,
however, with those rays which enter the substance
and impinge upon its inner or second surface; for
these at a particular angle of incidence undergo total
reflexion, so that none of the rays are transmitted at
the second surface. The angle of total reflexion is
constant for the same medium, but different for different media: thus in crown glass it is equal to about
40°, in flint-glass 38°, &c.; and this internal reflexion
from the second surface of transparent media is more
perfect than that occurring at the surface of opake
reflecting surfaces or mirrors.

If the reflecting surface be concave, as in Pl. XII.
fig. 4, parallel rays will be reflected to a focus a, nearer
the mirror than the centre of its curvature b, and this
focus is called the principal focus; while diverging
rays are brought to a focus nearer the centre of curvature; and converging rays form a focus further
from the centre of curvature.

Lenses.—In most instances, as far as the microscope
is concerned, the surfaces of the glass through which
the rays of light are transmitted are not plane or flat,
but curved—being either convex or concave, and belonging to convex or concave lenses. In considering
the course of rays through curved surfaces, the refraction may be viewed as taking place at a plane
surface forming a tangent at the point of incidence of

each ray; or each curved surface may be regarded as consisting of a number of minute plane surfaces placed at right angles to the perpendicular. Thus, in Pl. XII. fig. 5, the ray *a*, incident at the point *b* of the curved surface, is refracted towards the perpendicular *p*, as if it had fallen upon the plane surface represented by the tangent *t*. The forms of the most common lenses are represented in Pl. XII. figs. 6–10; —fig. 6 being doubly convex, or both surfaces being convex; fig. 7, plano-convex, or one surface plane, the other convex; fig. 8, doubly concave, or both surfaces being concave; fig. 9, plano-concave, one surface being plane, the other concave; and fig. 10 is a meniscus, in which one surface is convex and the other concave. The curved surfaces of lenses are usually portions of spheres.

The manner in which the course of a ray may be traced through a lens is illustrated by Pl. I. fig. 11, which requires no explanation after what has been already stated.

To facilitate the comprehension of the general action of lenses, they may be regarded as composed of two triangular prisms, with their bases in contact in a convex lens, as in fig. 12; their apices being opposed in a concave lens, as in fig. 13.

The point to which the rays converge after passing through a convex lens is called the *focus* (Pl. XII. fig. 14 *f*), the distance of which from the centre of the lens, called the focal length, obviously depends upon the direction of the incident rays. When these are parallel, which those coming from distant objects may be considered to be, the focus at which they meet is called the principal focus, or the focus for parallel rays: thus, in Pl. XII. fig. 14, the parallel rays meet at *f*, which is the principal focus.

If the incident rays are convergent, as in Pl. XII. fig. 15, the focus *o* will be situated nearer the lens than the principal focus, *f*. If, on the other hand, they are divergent, as in Pl. XII. fig. 16, the focus *f* will be situated further from the lens than the principal focus *o*.   By concave lenses the incident rays are rendered divergent, as in Pl. XII. fig. 17, as if they emanated from a point *f*, situated on the same side of the lens as that upon which the rays are incident, and called the virtual focus.

Spherical aberration.—Although, as a general expression, we have stated that the rays of light meet at a focus on passing through a convex lens, this is not strictly correct.   For, in ordinary convex lenses, the marginal rays are more refracted than the central ones, and meet at focal points nearer the lens than the latter, as shown in Pl. XII. fig. 18.   This important defect is called spherical aberration, and arises from the lateral rays being incident upon more oblique portions of the curved surface of the lens than the central rays.   Hence objects seen through such lenses appear misty and confused, the central and lateral parts of a flat object not being visible at the same time; and even when the marginal parts are visible, they appear distorted or deformed.

Spherical aberration is greatest in the most convex lenses; and, in a plano-convex lens, it is least when parallel rays enter at or emerge from its convex surface.

In certain lenses, the convex surface of which has the form of a parabola, a hyperbola, or an ellipse, the spherical aberration is absent; but it is impossible to grind microscopic lenses of these forms with absolute accuracy, so that the fact is of no practical value.

The form of simple convex lens most free from aberration is that in which the curves of the two surfaces form parts of a sphere, the radii of the curves being as 1 to 6; the focal length being rather less than twice the length of the radius of the most convex surface.   This form of lens comes very near to a plano-convex lens, which is consequently the best form for a simple lens.

Dispersion, or Chromatic Aberration.—The rays of light have so far been considered as simple. They are, however, in reality compound, consisting of a number of primary-coloured rays, of which seven kinds are easily distinguishable, viz. red, orange, yellow, green, blue, indigo, and violet. The coloured rays of the sun are, as is well known, often seen separated by the action of the triangular glass bars or prisms forming the lustres of a chandelier; the separation arising from the different refrangibility of the coloured rays, by which each is refracted to a different degree from that of the others. This is shown in Pl. XII. fig. 19, representing a ray of white light entering a triangular prism, at the surface of which the paths of the rays become different according to the degree of their refrangibility, whence they emerge separately, forming a *spectrum* at *v r*; the most refrangible violet rays (*v*) being most refracted, the less refrangible red (*r*) least so, the intermediate rays being refracted to intermediate degrees according to their respective refrangibilities. This separation of the coloured rays is called dispersion; and as different substances or media disperse the coloured rays over a larger or smaller space, so as to produce spectra of different lengths, they are said to possess different dispersive powers. Thus the dispersive power of flint glass and balsam are about equal, while that of crown glass is considerably less.

The extent to which dispersion is produced by the same medium also depends upon the angle of the prism, being greater as the angle is larger; increased obliquity of the incident light also increases the dispersion, so that the spectrum produced by a small prism may be equal to that produced by a larger one upon which the light is less obliquely incident.

In consequence of the dispersion of light, rays passing through a convex lens do not meet at a single point or focus (Pl. XII. fig. 20), but form as many foci as there are coloured rays.

When the spectrum is received upon a convex lens, the coloured rays are brought to a focus, and the light appears again white; for it is only when the primary-coloured rays are parallel, and seen close together, that they produce the impression of white or colour-less light. The spectra produced by different disper-sive media not only differ in length, but also in the breadth of the coloured spaces not being in the same ratio to each other; hence the spectra are said to be irrational, or the dispersion is said to be irrational.

Vision.—The visibility of an object depends upon the rays of light which emanate from each point of its surface presented to the eye being brought to a focus upon the ret'ina or expansion of the nerve of sight lining the inside of the back of the eye; so that, an image of each point being impressed upon the re-tina, the sum of the images forms the compound image of the entire object.

The manner in which the image is formed is shown in Pl. XII. fig. 21, in which, to prevent con-fusion, the rays coming from three points of the arrow only have been represented. The rays diverging from these three points, *a b c,* form cones in contact by their bases; the apex of each cone outside the eye being situated at the points *a b c,* the common base of each being situated at the crystalline lens *x,* im-mediately behind the pupil or rounded aperture in the coloured curtain of the eye, called the iris, *i i,* and which limits the base of the cones. The apices of the cones within the eye, *a'b'c',* are formed by the rays brought to foci upon the retina by the crystalline lens. The marginal cones of rays coming from the object cross within the eye, so that the uppermost rays from the object become lowermost upon the retina, and thus an inverted image of the object is formed. This appears to the eye to be erect, because the eye or rather the mind judges the parts of an object to be situated in that direction in which the rays coming from them are impressed upon it. Hence, as in fig. 21, the rays impressed upon the retina at the lower part a', appear to come from the upper part of the cross, although they are lowermost in the image, and so on for the other rays. For distinct vision the rays of each cone must be parallel, or nearly so.

Angle of Vision.—The marginal rays coming from the object cross at a point corresponding to the centre of the pupil, and thus form an angle, as seen in fig. 22, where the cones are omitted, to avoid confusion; this angle is the angle of vision. Now the size which objects appear to possess is measured by this angle, or by the linear magnitude of their images (*i. e.* their size estimated in one direction, as of length or breadth) upon the retina. When the object is distant, the angle and its linear magnitude are small, and it appears small and distant; whilst if it be large, or if small and brought near the eye, the reverse will be the case.

Magnification.—Hence an object may be made to appear larger, or may be magnified, by increasing the linear magnitude of its image upon the retina, which can be done by bringing it nearer the eye, as shown in fig. 22, where the image of b formed at b' is larger than the image of a formed at a'. But when an object is brought nearer the eye than about 8 or 10 inches (for the distance varies with different persons), its image becomes indistinct and misty; and this because the rays composing the cones are too divergent to meet at a focus upon the retina, as shown in fig. 23. By interposing a convex lens, however, between the eye and the object, the too divergent rays may be made to meet at a focus upon the retina, as in fig. 24, the object at the same time being rendered apparently larger or magnified, from the refracting action of the lens upon the cones.

Aplan'atism (*a*, not, πλανάω, to wander).—The effect of spherical aberration in rendering the image of an object seen through a lens indistinct and misty may now be intelligible. In order that such image may be distinct, the rays emanating from each point of the object must converge at one spot upon the retina. But since, when spherical aberration exists, the marginal rays are more refracted than the central ones, they will meet at foci before those formed by the latter; and when the foci of one set are coincident with the retina, so that the image would otherwise be distinct, the latter is rendered confused and indistinct by the rays of the other set.

In this consideration, we imply that there are only two sets of rays, the central and the marginal; but the central and marginal rays are not separate, for the rays possess every intermediate degree of obliquity, hence the foci and images are really innumerable.

Now there are evidently two methods of destroying or correcting spherical aberration, viz. by excluding the marginal rays, or by altering their direction.

The exclusion of the marginal rays is often adopted; and is effected by means of a diaphragm, or stop as it is called. This consists of a plate of metal, with a round aperture in the middle, and it is placed behind the lens; but it has the serious defect of diminishing considerably the amount of light transmitted.

The alteration of the direction of the marginal rays is produced by refraction, a thin plano-concave lens being placed in front of the convex one (Pl. XII. fig. 25). The doubly convex lens is composed of crown glass, and the concave lens of flint glass, which has a higher refractive and dispersive power than crown glass. In this way we get a compound lens, which, if the two lenses had the same refractive power, would simply amount to a plano-concave lens with the marginal portions removed. But as the concave lens consists of more highly refracting material than the convex, if the curve and thickness of the two lenses be properly adapted, the marginal portions of the concave correct the too great convergence of the marginal rays produced by the convex lens, and so the rays are brought to nearly the same focus. An idea of this action may be obtained from fig. 25, the dotted lines indicating the direction which the rays would take, if passing through the convex lens only.

A lens in which the spherical aberration is corrected is said to be aplanatic.

Achrómatism.—Supposing the spherical aberration of a lens to be corrected, there still remains the chromatic aberration (p. 173); for although the central or mean coloured rays may meet at a focus, the other coloured rays belonging to the same compound or ordinary ray will meet at different foci, so that a series of coloured images of the object will be formed at different distances from the lens; hence, at whichever focus the object is viewed, it will appear coloured.

Now the coloured primary rays can only be made to coincide in direction, so that the light parts of an object may appear white, by refraction. And the correction is produced by the same plano-concave lens as that which corrects the spherical aberration. But in this case the relative dispersive powers of the media composing the convex and the concave lenses form the point to be considered. If the dispersive power of the media of which the convex and concave lenses are composed were the same, the dispersive power of the convex lens would be in excess, and the coloured rays in each compound ray could not become parallel. But by forming the concave lens of a more highly dispersive medium, with a less proportional mean refraction than the convex, when the curves of the surfaces and the relative thickness of the lenses are properly adjusted, the dispersive action of the concave lens may be made equal to that of the convex; and being exerted in the opposite direction, the coloured rays will become parallel and meet at a single focus.

This may be elucidated by considering the lenses as composed of prisms. Thus, let fig. 28 represent the compound lens, the two halves of the doubly convex lens acting as two triangular prisms (fig. 19) with their bases opposed, converging the compound white rays *w w*, and dispersing the coloured elementary rays, which would form spectra at *s s*. In the plano-concave lens the triangular prisms may be considered as placed with their apices towards each other, and so would tend to disperse the coloured rays in the opposite direction, to form spectra at *t t*. Then, supposing the dispersions to be equal and in opposite directions, the coloured rays would become parallel and meet at a definite focus, the colour being destroyed. At the same time, the spherical action of the concave lens being opposite to that of the convex, the converging action of the latter will be diminished, so that the focus of the compound lens will be longer than that of the convex alone; but as the dispersive power of the concave is greater relatively than that of the convex, the mean refraction is less altered than the refraction or dispersion of the separate coloured rays; so that the concave wholly opposes or corrects the dispersion produced by the convex, while it only partially corrects its mean refraction.

A lens in which the chromatic and spherical aberrations are corrected or destroyed is commonly called achromatic; although the term properly applies to the correction of the colour only.

If in a compound lens the chromatic aberration is only partially corrected, so that the red rays still meet at a focus beyond the violet, as in a simple uncorrected lens (fig. 20), the lens is said to be under-corrected, or the aberration to be positive; while if the correcting action of the plano-concave lens be too great, so that the violet rays meet before the red, as in a simple concave lens, the lens is said to be over-corrected, and the aberration is called negative. Although the positive chromatic aberration of the extreme rays passing through a convex lens may be corrected by the negative aberration of a concave lens, there still remains a certain amount of uncorrected colour, arising from the irrationality of the spectra of the two refracting media. This evil cannot be overcome, and the remaining colour is said to arise from the secondary spectrum.

The object-glasses of the microscope, consisting of the compound lenses, have their aberrations balanced to a considerable extent on the above principles—the lowest combination being under-corrected, while the upper combinations are over-corrected; and, by suitable adaptation of their distance from each other, further correction may be obtained, the aberration of the object-glass altogether being, however, over-corrected or negative.

The eye-piece consists of two simple plano-convex lenses, the upper or eye-glass (fig. 27 e) having a shorter focus than the lower (f) or field-glass, and the two placed at the distance of half the sum of their focal lengths. The object-glass alone would form an enlarged and reversed image of the object within the body of the microscope, the cones of rays from each point of the object terminating at the larger arrows in the figure (fig. 27). But the rays meeting the field-glass are brought by it to a focus at the position of the smaller arrows, where they form a reduced image; and, subsequently passing through the eye-glass, they are so altered in direction as to enter the eye at a greater angle, and to present a magnified image of the object.

The eye-piece produces several important effects. The refraction being produced by two less convex lenses instead of one of greater convexity, the spherical aberration is considerably reduced; and the convexities of the lenses in the eye-piece being situated in an opposite direction to that of those in the object-glass, the spherical aberration of the former reverses and so neutralizes that of the latter. Also the under-correction of the field-glass compensates the over-correction of the object-glass—the blue rays which are refracted more than the red by the field-glass, being thrown upon the eye-glass nearer its centre, where the refraction is less, and thus the coloured rays become parallel or nearly so on reaching the eye. Moreover the field-glass collects a larger number of rays than the eye-glass could do alone, so that it enlarges the field and increases its brightness.

In the best object-glasses the aberrations are so well balanced that the mere covering an object with thin glass is sufficient to disturb the balance and render very delicate markings either misty and coloured or wholly invisible. The effect produced by a plate of glass may be understood by reference to fig. 26, the rays being supposed to emanate from the object at a; and it is evident that the refraction of the glass so alters the direction of the rays that they will fall upon the lower combination nearer the centre than if the cover were absent, and thus negative aberration is produced. In the best object-glasses, however, this aberration may almost entirely be removed, the lower combination being susceptible of approximation by a screw movement to the second or next above it, so that the ascending rays, being able to continue their oblique course through the increased distance between the object and the lower combination, may fall upon the same portions of the latter that they did before the cover was applied.

POLARIZATION OF LIGHT.—In attempting to give a sketch of this curious and difficult subject, we must suppose the reader to be in possession of a natural crystal of calcareous spar, and either two Nicol's prisms (forming the ordinary polariscope) or two plates of the mineral called tourmaline cut in the direction of the length or axis of the crystal.

Hitherto we have considered rays of light falling upon transparent substances as simply refracted or reflected according to the ordinary laws of refraction or reflexion. We have now to notice some curious exceptions, forming the basis of many interesting phenomena, especially in connexion with the microscope, in which these laws are more or less deviated from. If we place a plate of tourmaline, cut as above directed, upon or beneath the stage of the microscope, the light will pass through it, appearing tinged with the green or brown colour natural to the tourmaline; but on laying another slice upon the eye-piece, and turning the latter round or rotating it, the light will be transmitted in certain positions only, being partially or entirely arrested in others, so that the field appears black. And, on careful examination, it will be noticed that the change from black to white occurs at each quarter of a rotation, being twice black and twice white in an entire rotation, the changes occurring alternately. The same phenomena may also be exhibited by substituting two Nicol's prisms for the tourmalines.

Again, if we take a natural crystal of calcareous spar, and paste upon one side of it a piece of black paper with a small hole in the middle, on holding the crystal to the light or over a piece of white paper, with the covered side next the light, two holes or two images of the hole will be seen; and if the crystal without the paper be placed over some print, the print will appear double. Hence the light passing through the hole is twice or doubly refracted, one ray following the ordinary law of refraction, while the other follows a different law, being retarded and pursuing a longer course; and so the two rays are called respectively the ordinary and extraordinary ray. And on viewing

R

these through a tourmaline or a Nicol's prism, as in the experiment with the two tourmalines, the images will become alternately visible and invisible, just as was then the case with the entire mass of light.

The light which has undergone this singular change is said to be polarized, because the rays appear to have acquired poles or sides. In the above experiments the lower prism or tourmaline is called the polarizer, because it polarizes the light, and the upper is called the analyzer, because it analyzes or tests the light altered by the former.

An idea of the cause of this change may be obtained by reference to the undulatory theory of light. Ordinary light consists of waves or undulations taking place in planes at right angles to each other, or in all planes; while in polarized light the undulations are all in one plane or in parallel planes. This may perhaps be understood by considering that books in a book-case are situated in parallel planes, the shelves being in planes at right angles to the former. And by imagining in polarizing substances the existence of some structure acting like a grating, a notion can be obtained how the rays in the different planes may be transmitted or intercepted. If the grating be so placed that the bars (representing the planes of polarization) are perpendicular, the books can pass between them; while if the grating be turned round a quarter of a circle, they will become transverse, and the books cannot pass, while the shelves could do so. Carrying on this analogy, the tourmaline or Nicol's prism polarizes the light by transmitting only those rays whose undulations are in planes parallel to the bars; while the analyzer allows these undulations to pass through it when the direction of the planes coincides with that of the bars, but interrupts them when their direction is at right angles to the bars. And it is evident that the planes of polarization of the ordinary and extraordinary rays are opposite, from the opposite action of the analyzer upon them.

The power of doubly refracting and polarizing is not possessed by all crystalline bodies, but only those belonging to other than the cubic system; crystals belonging to this system neither doubly refract nor polarize light. In all doubly refracting crystals there are one or more lines or directions in which the light is not doubly refracted. These are called the optic axes, and sometimes they coincide with the geometric axis of the crystals, at others they do not; and they may be regarded as positions or directions of equilibrium of certain molecular forces existing within the crystal, which, acting in opposition, neutralize each other.

If light, polarized by the polarizer, be transmitted through thin doubly refracting crystals, and analyzed by the analyzer, splendid colours will become visible; and on rotating separately either the polarizer or the analyzer, at each quarter rotation the colours will change, being complementary to those at first visible, or such as are requisite with the first to make white light. We have seen (fig. 19) that white light consists of seven coloured rays, or of three primary colours—red, yellow, and blue, which, by superposition, form the others; and thus red is complementary to green, which consists of blue and yellow, the two sets of complementary colours appearing and vanishing as the light and darkness did when the crystals were not used.

These colours are produced by interference. The compound rays of white light (fig. 30 *l*) passing through the polarizer (*t*) are all polarized in one plane; the crystal (*d*) depolarizes this light, *i. e.* doubly refracts and resolves it into two sets of rays polarized in planes at right angles to each other, forming the ordinary, o, and the extraordinary ray, E. Each of these two sets of rays is resolved by the analyzer (*s*) into two other sets, polarized in planes at right angles to each other; so that in all there are four sets, two in one plane and two in the other; and, the primary rays of the two sets in each plane being in different stages or phases of undulation, in consequence of the retardation of the extraordinary rays, the undulations of certain coloured rays check and annihilate each other, while the remainder or complementary conspire and pursue their course, producing the appearance of colour, this effect being reversed at each quarter-revolution of the analyzer.

An idea of what is meant by phases of undulation may be obtained by reference to fig. 29, in which the undulations, *a, b,* are in similar states or phases, and so conspire in action, while the wave *c* is in a different phase and half an undulation behind the others; hence it would check or interfere with either of the other waves (*a, b*), the etherial molecules of the two, which vibrate perpendicularly or at right angles to the direction of the wave, acting to the same extent and in opposite directions.

In fig. 30 the analyzer is represented as composed of a natural crystal (rhomb) of calcareous spar, which transmits both sets of rays; but in the ordinary analyzer or Nicol's prism—which is made by dividing a rhomb through the obtuse angles into two wedge-shaped pieces and cementing them together again with balsam, only one set of rays is transmitted at each quarter-revolution, the other being refracted out of the field. In the case of the tourmaline, one of the sets of rays is absorbed; so that the tourmaline, like the Nicol's prism, is single-imaged.

Thus the colours produced by polarization are the same as those of the spectrum, but separated in a different way, both arising from the elementary coloured rays of the compound white light. For while the spectral rays are separated by dispersive refraction, the polarized coloured rays are separated by the interference and annihilation of some rays, the remainder passing on to produce the colours.

When the position of the depolarizing crystal is such that the plane of the polarized light coincides with the direction of the optic axis or axes, the light is not doubly refracted nor polarized in certain parts; hence these parts appear white if the plane of the polarizer and analyzer coincide, and black if they be crossed. A crystal cut at right angles to its optic axis, with its length directed towards the polarizer and analyzer, is in this position, and it exhibits alternately a black and white cross, with one or two sets of concentric rings of complementary colours at each quarter of a rotation.

To prepare crystals for examination by polarized light, a little Epsom salt, nitre, or borax should be dissolved in water, a drop placed upon a slide, and dried at a gentle heat. The crystals should then be mounted in balsam, and viewed as transparent objects.

To see the cross and rings, the crystals should be sawn or cut across transversely, the ends being polished on a strained piece of silk moistened with water, and the sections mounted in balsam.

The property of doubly refracting and polarizing light is not confined to crystalline substances, being also possessed by many organic bodies, for the details of which I must refer to the article Polarization in the 'Micrographic Dictionary.'

INDEX.

www.ingramcontent.com/pod-product-compliance
Lightning Source LLC
Chambersburg PA
CBHW030402270326
41926CB00009B/1236